Rich Buyer,
Rich Seller!

D0958206

Rich Buyer, Rich Seller!

The Real Estate Agents' Guide to Marketing Luxury Homes

Laurie Moore-Moore

National Speaker and Consultant
President, Institute for Luxury Home Marketing

10   9   8   7   6   5   4   3   2   1

Book design and production by Bookwrights Design

Jacket design by Michael Komarck

Printed in the United States of America

Library of Congress Cataloging-in-Publication Data
on file with the Publisher

ISBN 0-9726001-0-8

Institute for Luxury Home Marketing
1409 South Lamar # 355
Dallas, Texas 75215-1871
(214) 485-3000

Dedication

For the two men who make my life richer
by their presence

Roger, the love of my life
Waco, our wonderful son who always makes us proud

Contents

Introduction

This book begins with information gathering about the upper tier market, about affluent prospects, about your competitors, and about the skills you need to work with the affluent. I believe if you are knowledgeable about these things you enhance your probability of success. There are also lots of marketing ideas, and tips for helping you secure the upper-priced listing, capture buyer prospects, and sell properties. I hope you will enjoy reading this book and find it to be a useful tool as you work with rich buyers, rich sellers, and ultra consumers.

May your real estate successes bring you happiness and affluence.

Chapter 1

The Importance of Information Gathering

Over the past five or six years I've trained more than 6,000 agents in luxury home marketing. Invariably, agents tell me that two of the stories that I share in my presentations are important in reinforcing the critical importance of information gathering for success. So, I decided to share them with you as well.

Story One

I've learned a lot about business from my young nephew. When he was born he was named Paul Powell IV. His dad is Paul Powell III. We call his dad P3. So, the obvious name for this new little guy was P4. We called this child P4 for about three years and then it became readily apparent that this was not the right name for him. P4 was a going concern; he was into everything; he never slowed down; he had a zillion questions. He was turbo-charged. So we began to call him Turbo.

One day when Turbo was not quite four years old, he was outside with his dad. It was a hot Texas summer day and they were working on a father-and-son project —washing the car. The dad, P3, was soaping away and Turbo's job was rinsing the car with the hose.

If you've been around a three- or a four-year-old, you know the attention span is short. Sure enough, it wasn't long before Turbo became bored rinsing the car. He spun around and began to water a flowerbed where nothing was planted yet, just freshly turned soil. After about a minute, a frog popped up. Turbo's eyes got really big. He turned around to his dad and said, "Dad, I just *made* a frog!" His dad laughed and went on soaping the car. Meanwhile, Turbo began watering the flower bed with a vengeance and it didn't take very long before POP! POP! up popped two more frogs. Turbo turned back around and said, "Dad, I made two more frogs and it's easy: all you do is add water to dirt."

This is a silly story. But when I heard it, I thought, "I've done that." I've done it more than once in my own business, and I'll bet you have too: We jump to the wrong conclusion because we don't have all the information. Turbo didn't know that in the hot Texas summer frogs burrow down into the ground to stay cool. It was the water that provided the impetus for those frogs to pop right up, but, because Turbo didn't have all the information, he mistakenly thought he'd *made* frogs.

Think about that in the context of your own real estate business. When you first came into real estate, did you step back and gather information and analyze the market to determine which market segments in which areas were the most active, or did you just jump in and start doing business? Most of us simply begin with little or no information gathering. And, after you've been at this business for several years, there's the temptation to think, "I understand this business; I've been doing it a long time."

But, as you know, the market changes.

Story Two

If you were in real estate in 1981, you witnessed significant changes in the industry. Interest rates soared — eighteen, nineteen, twenty percent rates were common — and in most markets, housing demand dwindled. In Dallas, rates were high but the market had so much corporate growth, including a couple of major corporate group moves, that real estate activity was high. Because Dallas was one of the few active residential real estate markets in the country in 1981, the money came to Dallas. The investors, lenders, builders, and developers swarmed into the market. If you could spell "builder", you could be one. If you could show you knew which end of the hammer to hold, you probably had savings and loan institutions or other investors lined up to joint venture with you. As a result, new home inventory exploded.

But it wasn't long before the group moves were over and corporate activity began to slow as corporations began to downsize (or "right-size" as they prefer to call it). The oil industry cratered (oil is a small percentage of Dallas' economy, but at that point any healthy business would have helped). Suddenly real estate agents looked at the market and said, "Uh oh, we're going to have to tighten our belts, because times are going to be tough for a while in real estate in Dallas." The signs were there: Inventory was up and demand was down.

There was one real estate agent in Dallas who looked around and said, "You know, I've been doing this a long time, and if I've learned anything, it's that no matter what goes on in the market there's always an opportunity. The trick is finding it." So she began to do a little information gathering. She analyzed the market and said to herself, "I think I see the opportunities. All these builders of all these speculatively built new homes are not going to be able to sell them. There are going to be savings and loans, mortgage companies, and other investors foreclosing on those properties. Institutions don't want to hold homes in their portfolios."

Then she realized, "I've handled a lot of new homes, I understand the new home product and I've worked with a lot of third party companies so I understand the institutional seller. I must be a new homes institutional expert." She began to go around and call on the S&Ls. She would tell them, "I know you're getting ready to foreclose on some new homes. You don't want to hold those homes in your portfolio. Call me; I can help you sell them. I'm a new homes institutional expert."

In the first twelve months of pursuing this strategy, she sold and closed more than $30 million worth of residential real estate. That's not a shabby number in any market. When others were complaining about their worst year in real estate, the agent who took the time to gather information found the opportunity for tremendous success.

This story is important for two reasons. First, it is a reminder that no matter what happens in the market there is always an opportunity. Second, it highlights (like Turbo and the frog) the importance of information gathering. One goal of this book is to help you gather the information and ideas that will help you be successful in luxury home marketing.

Chapter 2

Why Work in the Upper Tier?

Working in the upper tier has its advantages.

1. There's **a higher income potential**. Since commission is based on a percentage of the selling price, a more expensive property generates a higher commission.
2. **There are fewer competitors in the upper tier**. Many agents are intimidated by the idea of working with the wealthy. They say, "I just don't know if I'd be comfortable working with somebody who lives in a million-dollar house." Money, power, and fame can be intimidating, and that keeps some agents out of the luxury home arena.
3. **The upper tier buyer or seller is often more resistant to economic change** than prospects in the average price range. They are often less affected by fluctuations in interest rates. Many times they're all-cash buyers. Some are sophisticated investors who understand the real estate market and may invest in homes as part of their overall investment strategy.

The housing market during the economic slowdown of 2000 illustrates the resilience of the affluent consumer. Purchases of lower end homes ($119,000 and below) dropped 11.2 % in 2000 as compared to 1999 as low- to middle-income households felt the economic pinch. On the other hand, the sales of homes in the $400,000 and above price range increased a whopping 22.2% to a total of 7.3 % of all homes sold. Sales continued to be strong in the $400,000 price range across most of the country in 2001 and 2002 started with healthy upper tier sales in most markets.

National Association of Realtors' Research Economist Kevin Thorpe explained the upper tier's resilience in an article entitled "Home Buying Trends—High-end Homes," in the April 2001 issue of **Real Estate Outlook**. "Those in the higher income bracket generally look to buy pricier homes, and given their financial stability, are less sensitive to economic downcycles. In addition, the volatility in the stock market prompted many wealthy investors to turn to the real estate sector to add stability to their portfolio."

4. There is a **great deal of personal satisfaction** associated with being a successful agent in the upper tier. If you're successful in the luxury market, you probably have knowledge and competencies over and above that of the average agent, and that can be satisfying.

5. Your peers recognize that to succeed in the higher price ranges, you have to be good. Often **peer recognition** or status is associated with being successful in the luxury home market.

The luxury market offers challenges, too

Although there are lots of positives associated with targeting the luxury home niche, you must also recognize some not-so-positive realities.

1. **Not every upper-tier listing sells**. In fact, as price goes up, conversion tends to go down. So, there's a risk involved for the agent who must invest time and money in marketing each property.

2. **Expensive homes usually take longer to sell**. That adds to the risk. Be sure to educate your seller regarding

expected sales time based on the property price.

3. **It costs more to market an expensive property**. The marketing plan required to give an upper priced property the targeted exposure necessary to sell it can be expensive. High quality brochures, targeted mailing lists, regional or national media exposure, special open house events, and other marketing tools require a significant marketing budget. Generally, you expect to invest more to sell a fine home or estate property. Marketing time is also an issue since a longer sales period may mean more marketing dollars spent. Creativity and good networking will help you keep marketing costs affordable.

4. **You are dealing with some of the most demanding buyers and sellers**. You have to be prepared to communicate effectively and deliver high quality customer service. To be successful in the luxury home market, you have to be knowledgeable and skillful. You must know your market, understand the buying/selling process, and be committed to delivering quality customer service. You must take the time to understand your clients' wants and needs and clarify their expectations. Let them know how you work, what expectations you have of them, and what to expect from the home buying or selling process. Then, educate them about the market, keep communication open, and deal with problems promptly. After the fact, ask for a service evaluation to measure how well you did. And, don't forget to ask for testimonials and referrals.

5. Although you'll encounter fewer competitors in the high price ranges, the agents you are competing with are good and **competition is keen**. Your skills need to be sharp if you expect to be competitive.

6. Sometimes expensive homes result in **more complex transactions**. Occasionally they're easier —an all-cash transaction can sometimes be simple. But other play-

ers sometimes appear when you work in the upper tier. These other players can add complexity. Here's an example.

In the Midwest not long ago I was talking to an agent who said, "Laurie, I just did the most complex listing presentation that I've ever done."

I asked, "What made it complex?"

He said, "Well first of all, although the home is located here in my city in the Midwest, I did the listing presentation in the board room of a skyscraper in Manhattan using my laptop and an LCD projector."

This made me curious, "Why did you have to do that?"

"Well," he said, "the woman who owned the home died and the property went into a family trust. Present at the listing presentation in New York were the following people —the New York-based trustee, the family banker, the family accountant, heir number one and his spouse, heir number two and her business manager, heir number three and his agent. There were nine people present, and each one seemed to have a different perspective. I got the listing, but, now I'm a bit apprehensive about the contracting process. "

The agent is right to be concerned. Do you suppose those nine people have the same agenda with regard to the sale of that property? Probably not. If the listing presentation was complex, what's the contract negotiation going to be like? Unless somebody has been designated as responsible for the negotiation of the contract, the transaction has the potential to be very complicated. Even if one person is selected to negotiate the sale, there are probably going to be lots of things going on below the surface of that negotiation that will continue to make it complex. People skills and good communication will be important attributes for the listing agent.

All in all, if you target the upper-tier market, you must recognize up front that you will probably have to invest more time and more marketing dollars. But, remember, the financial rewards are greater, too. Expect to be patient with luxury buyers; they often move slowly and may have to wait for just the right house to come on the market (inventory is smaller). You may encounter additional players who add complexity to the transaction. On the other hand, if you are dealing with an all-cash transaction, you may find the contract-to-closing process is faster because financing isn't an issue.

Chapter 3

Defining and Measuring the Upper-Tier Market

The definition of the upper-tier residential real estate market (what we might call the rich buyer/rich seller market) varies depending upon location.

For the purposes of this book, we can say that the upper-tier market in any given area is the top 10 percent of residential home sales based on price OR $400,000, whichever is *higher*.

The $400,000 figure is a floor for the upper tier since in small markets the top 10 percent of sales might actually be below $400,000. On the other end of the scale, in many markets, the top 10 percent of residential sales will be priced significantly higher than $400,000.

According to Worth Magazine, which ranks communities based on median home prices (the mid point), there are more than 250 communities where the top half of the residential home sales exceeds $400,000. The pricey *Top Five Towns* on Worth's list for 2001 are significantly more expensive:

Community	Median Home Price	Population
Jupiter Island (FL)	$3,937,500	601
Atherton (CA)	$2,697,500	7,500
Aspen (CO)	$2,300,000	5,049
Los Altos Hills (CA)	$2,100,000	7,900
Belvedere (CA)	$1,824,500	2,071

Source: *Worth* Magazine, "America's Richest Towns of 2001: By Median Home Price"

The Size of the National Upper-Tier Home Market

Despite the fact that there are some very expensive communities, the luxury home market is a small segment of the total number of homes in the United States, so luxury homes are a small proportion of the homes sold each year.

Home Values of Owner Occupied Homes in the U.S.

Home Value	% Homes	Number of Homes
$ 300,000—$ 499,999	6.5 %	3,584,000
$ 500,000—$ 999,999	2.4 %	1,306,000
$1,000,000 and above	.6 %	314,000

Source: Census Bureau, Profile of Selected Home Characteristics, 2000

Percentage of homes sold at $400,000 or above

1999	5.8 %
2000	7.3 %

Source: NAR Research Division

Percentage of homes sold at $500,000 or above	
1st Quarter 2001	4.7 %
4th Quarter 2001	4.9 %
1st Quarter 2002	5.5 %

Source: NAR Research Division

If we analyze household income, it is easy to understand why upper-tier home sales are such a small percentage of total home sales.

According to the most current U.S. Census Bureau report, the median income for all U.S. households is $41,994. (Remember that the median is the middle point: half the households earn more, half earn less.) So it should come as no surprise that the government views you as affluent if your total household income is as much as $100,000 annually.

In some expensive housing markets, this level of income may not be enough to guarantee you entry into the luxury home market. Nonetheless, households earning *at least* $100,000 represent only 12.3 of all of the country's estimated 106 million households and only about 2.4 percent of all households earn as much as $200,000 annually. (NOTE: Some of the Census Bureau information relates to households that earn income —as compared to ALL households. The percentage of these "income households" earning at least $100,000 is 13.3%.

U.S. Household Income Estimates	
Income	**% of All Households**
$ 75,000 - $ 99,999	10.2 %
$100,000 - $149,999	7.7 %
$150,000 - $199,999	2.2 %
$200,000 and up	2.4 %
Percentage earning $100,000 or more 12.3%	

Source: Census Bureau, Profile of Selected Economic Characteristics, 2000

The good news is that Americans are becoming more affluent. In the past two decades, the growth in the number of households earning $100,000 (in inflation-adjusted dollars) has outpaced the total growth in households. Unless we have a dramatic decline in the economy, the fact that tens of thousands of baby boom households (with heads of households ranging from 38 to 56) are moving into prime earning years should create even more households with $100,000 income.

Number of $100,000 *Income* Households And The Percent of Total Households They Represent

Year	All Households (HH)	Number $100,000	HH/Percent HH
1980	82.4 million	4.5 million	5.5 %
1990	94.3 million	8.0 million	8.5 %
1999	104.7 million	12.8 million	12.2 %
2000*	106.4 million	4.2 million	13.3 %*

Source: U.S. Census Bureau

* *Census Bureau, Selected Characteristics of Households by Total Money Income in 2000. Current Population Survey.* November 2001 weighting correction

Fast Facts about households earning $100,000 plus.
- The median age of the heads of households earning at least $100,000 is 47 —a baby boom household.
- Slightly more than three out of four of these households have two or more earners.
- Average household size is 3.25 people.
- Nine out of 10 own the homes in which they live*
- 37% Have equity in residential real estate other than a primary residence (second homes, time shares, or rental property with four or fewer units)*

- 23% have equity in non-residential real estate*
- 35% have ownership in privately held businesses*
- 88% are family households, 12% are singles or other non-family households.
- Geographic distribution of these households is fairly even

  South   31 %

  West 25 %

  Northeast   22 %

  Midwest   22 %

Source: *Census Bureau, Selected Characteristics of Households by Total Money Income in 2000. Current Population Survey.* Items with asterisks are from Survey of Consumer Finances, Published by the Board of Governors, Federal Reserve System.

The small percentage of households earning at least $100,000 explains why the luxury home market is a small segment of the total. The income and net worth groups which are prospects in the upper tier are discussed in chapter five.

Comparing Your Market to the Nation

Think about the top 10 percent of homes in your housing market and the income necessary to buy into that luxury home segment. Based on income, what percentage of total U.S. households would you estimate could afford to buy your latest luxury home listing? Although that's an interesting question, the more relevant question for a real estate agent working in the luxury home market is: How rich is your market?

To determine household income breakdowns in zip codes in your community, see *The Sourcebook—ZIP CODE Demographics* published by CACI and available in most large libraries in the business reference section. For instance, I looked up the 75075 zip code in the fast-growing metropolitan Dallas suburban market of Plano in *ZIP CODE Demographics* 2000. The table below will show you some of what I found.

Demographic Information for Zip Code 75075 in Plano (TX)

20,245 Households
16,124 Family Households
Percent of Households earning $100,000 or more = 37 %
Percent of households earning $150,000 or more = 12 %
Median household income = $81,529
This zip code is one of the most affluent in the country.
Median household income is in the top 2% of all U.S. zip codes

© The Sourcebook—ZIP CODE Demographics, 2000,CACI

For comparison, let's look at a zip code in another Dallas suburb.

Demographic Information for Zip Code 75040 in Garland (TX)

16,084 Households
11,785 Family Households
Percent of Households earning $100,000 or more = 11.1 %
Percent of Households earning $150,000 or more = 1.4 %
Median household income = $53,530
This zip code is more affluent than the average U.S. zip code
Median household income is in the top 13 % of all U.S. zip codes

Source: The Sourcebook— ZIP CODE Demographics, 2000, CACI

Even though households in both these zip codes in the same metropolitan market are more affluent than average, there is a substantial difference between them in terms of earnings in the $100,000 and above range. Take the time to analyze your market area by zip code. Share the resulting data with your sellers and use it to negotiate for your buyers.

Canadian household earnings

In 2000, the median household income in Canada was $51,000 (in Canadian dollars).

Income data is available broken down by letter carrier routes, census tracts, urban forward sortation areas (the first three characters of the postal code), cities, towns, federal electoral districts, census divisions, census metropolitan areas, economic regions, provinces, and territories. For more information, visit *www.statcan.ca* or call 866-652-8443 or 613-951-9720.

Chapter 4

Analyzing Your Local Upper Tier Market

Define your upper tier market and break it into price ranges

If you expect to be an expert in the upper-tier market, you must know and understand your market. In addition to having previewed the luxury home resale inventory and being familiar with the new home builders and their luxury home products, you must also take the time to gather and analyze the statistics relevant to the upper-tier market niche. Here are some steps to start your analysis of the market so you can position yourself as an expert and help your affluent prospects make better real estate decisions:

1. Define the geographic area that you serve —you personally, not your company, not your office.

2. Go into your multiple listing system database and identify the top 10 percent of properties sold in the last 12 months in your market area. This will define what the upper tier is in the market area in which you work.

3. Take the top 10 percent of closed properties and break it into logical price bands or price ranges. Different markets will have different price ranges. In some markets the breakdown of the top 10 percent of home sales might look like this:

  $400,00 - $499,999
  $500,000 - $749,999

$750,000 - $999,999
$1,000,000 - $1,499,999
$1,500,000 - $1,999,999
$2,000,000 and above

In very expensive markets, the top ten percent may start significantly higher than $400,000.

4. Once you have broken your market into logical price bands or price ranges, look at each price band and research the following:

- The sales to expiration ratio. (The percent that actually sells versus those that expire)

- The average days on market within each of those price bands.

- The list-to-sales-price differential (what did it list for, what did it sell for, what was the percentage of list price to sales price?)

- The approximate percentage of new homes on the market versus resale. You won't find this in MLS data; you'll have to estimate based on your market knowledge.

- The number of closed transactions in each price range or price band.

- The listing term that your competition is getting in each price range This statistic will be your "best guess" since MLS probably doesn't record this.

You are probably thinking that you already know these statistical averages for the total listing inventory in your MLS. But it's important to calculate these things for each of the price bands in the top ten percent, because the statistics will be different.

Once you have this information, how are you going to use it? Let's analyze the sample market that I have broken into price bands in the list above.

Days-on-market

Here is a sample chart tracking average days on market by price range for an imaginary market. Take your market's data to create your chart.

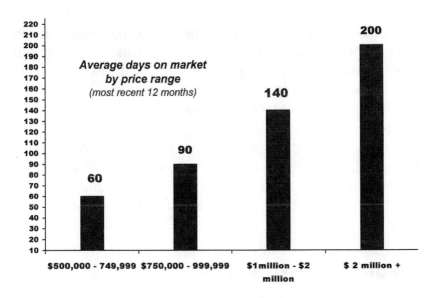

As you might have expected, the sample chart shows that it takes longer to sell the more expensive properties. How can you use the information? Assume you have someone whose property you believe should be listed just *under* $500,000. They, on the other hand, are convinced the home needs to be priced just *above* $500,000. There's a full month's difference in selling time between the two price ranges. For an expensive home, the costs associated with carrying that property for an extra month plus the inconvenience of a slower sale can be substantial, especially if your seller is transferring or trying to time a sale with the closing on another property. This statistic gives you the information you need to negotiate price more effectively with your seller. You may already be doing this using average statistics for the overall market, but it's much more powerful if you know exactly what is happening in the market by individual price range.

This data can also help you make better decisions. If you are listing a million-dollar property under the scenario shown by the chart above, you want more than a six-month listing. You wouldn't be satisfied with six months because it's not giving you even the average number of days on market for a property to sell in that price range. You'll want a longer listing term in order to have a fair chance to sell the property. Given the marketing costs associated with a million-dollar-plus listing, it can be an expensive proposition if your listing term is too short and the seller doesn't relist with you. Taking the time to analyze the market gives you the information to make good business decisions such as the listing term to request.

Average days on market will tell you the *minimum* listing term you want based on the probable sales price. Sharing this selling time expectation with the homeowner at the listing stage will also help your seller develop realistic expectations. This also can open a dialogue about the relationship between price and selling time.

List-to-sales-price ratio

Let's look at other ways this data can be valuable. Below I have I plotted the list–to-sales-price ratio for homes priced in the $500,000 to just under $750,000 price range for my imaginary market.

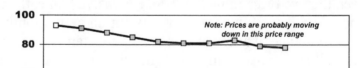

List-to-Sale Price Ratio for homes priced from $1,000,000 to $1,499,999

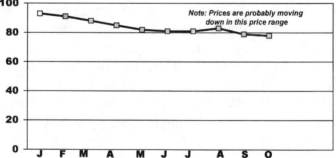

In this particular price range the list-to-sales-price ratio is slipping. Generally this would imply that that the prices of homes in this price band are declining. In this situation would you want to take a slightly overpriced listing? Obviously not, because the market's going to make it worse. If the line on the chart were trending up instead of down, that would indicate rising prices and you'd be more willing to take a slightly overpriced listing because the market would correct the overpricing over time. Certainly there would be some other factors to consider before taking an overpriced listing; however, if you know this information, you are much more likely to negotiate your list prices in a way that will give you the best opportunity to sell your listings. You can utilize this information with buyers as well as with sellers.

It is interesting that even in a market where prices are trending upward, you may have price ranges in the upper tier that are flat. If you take the time to analyze the market by price range you'll understand what's happening and be able to guide your prospects and make solid business decisions for yourself.

Buyers by price range

One of the most important bits of information to gather is the number of buyers by price range. On the chart below titled *Number of Buyers by Price Range*, I have simply plotted the number of homes sold and closed by price range in the last six months in an imaginary market. The same chart in your market might look very different, but the concept is what's important, not whether this is reflective of your marketplace. Notice the terminology; the chart's title refers to the number of *buyers* by price range. The number of sales (closed transactions) in each price range is the same as the number of buyers who actually purchased homes in that price range and closed on them. In this business, we typically talk about the number of properties sold or the number of sales, but let me ask you a question: If you list a $750,000 house does your seller believe that there are buyers on every corner? Usually the seller overestimates the demand in the market. But if you will track this statistic and make a simple change in terminology, it may help your seller recognize that buyers for high-priced homes may not be waiting on every corner.

Talk about *REAL BUYERS* as opposed to closed transactions or homes sold. Using "number of real buyers" instead of "number of sales" with your sellers can be a dose of reality. *"In the last 90 days, in the price range where you want to list your home, there have been six real buyers or two per month. And it has taken an average of 175 days of marketing to find each of those buyers."* That's powerful information!

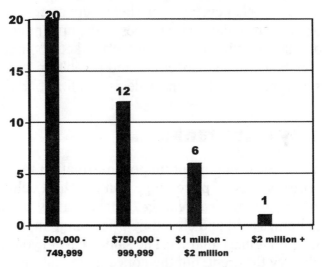

Number of buyers by price range in last 3 months

Here's a way to use this information. Let's assume you have a seller who wants to list at just over $750,000 and you think the list price needs to be a bit under $750,000. You can say to that seller, "In the last six months, in the price range where you would like to list your property, there has been one real buyer per month. However, if we keep it under $750,000 we are in a price range where there have been two buyers per month. We're doubling the odds of selling your home by listing it under $750,000." When you can justify why you are recommending a particular list price and show the seller specific statistics regarding the alternate price ranges, you are educating your seller to the reality of the market. You are also more likely to receive a properly priced listing.

Gather the statistics, change your terminology from "sales" to "number of real buyers," and take the time to make the charts so that you have a visual tool to use with your sellers. Recognize that you can also use this tool when you represent the buyer. It's very effective when you are presenting a contract to be able to show the listing agent and seller that, "There were only ten real buyers in this price range in the last month. My buyer is qualified, likes the house, and is ready to purchase. With so few buyers out there, doesn't it make sense to do this deal?"

The odds of selling your home

As you do your upper-tier market analysis, create a chart called "The Odds of Selling Your Home." In the sample below, I've broken a real market into price bands and I've pulled the MLS data on the number of listings in each price range as well as the number of properties sold (real buyers) in each price range over the past 90 days. Then, I've done a simple calculation, dividing the number sold by the number of listings. The resulting number is the odds of selling your home in that price range in the last 90 days. As you can see, the odds range from a low of 25 percent to a high of 77 percent.

It's interesting to note how the odds vary. In this market, the highest odds are not in the lowest price bands. The active segment in this particular market is $500,000 to $600,000. Doing this calculation identifies which price bands are the most active, and you can sit down with your sellers and talk about the actual odds of selling their home based on the current activity in their price range.

The Odds of Selling Your Home

Price	sold	for sale	odds
$350,000 - 499,999	106	181	59%
$500,000 - 599,999	138	179	77%
$600,000 - 649,999	87	185	47%
$750,000 - 999,999	73	132	55%
$1,000,000 - 1,499,999	10	30	33%
$1,500,000 - 1,999,999	4	16	25%
$2,000,000 +	2	8	25%

You can do this same statistic with pending sales, which gives you an even more current picture of the odds of selling your home. If you think your market conditions are changing, comparing sold statistics to pending statistics can be useful.

The sale-to-expiration ratio is also a useful statistic to track by price range. It illustrates the same trends in demand that the Odds of Selling Your Home calculations will reveal.

Where are your buyers coming from?

It is also useful to track —by price range —where your buyers are coming from. Doing this company-wide will give you valuable information that will help you market more effectively. Here's an example of how you might use the information:

An agent in Florida listed a million-dollar-plus property on a canal. On the shore of the canal was a boat slip that would accommodate a boat of up to 120 feet. Fortunately for this agent, her company tracks where their buyers come from. She knew that in the over $1 million price range, there was a 70 percent chance that her buyer would come from Florida or several states contiguous to Florida. Given the price of the property, she assumed that the buyer prospects for the home would need to be multi-millionaires. So, she rented a mailing list of multi-millionaires who lived in Florida and those relevant states contiguous to Florida and she further specified that she only wanted the ones who owned boats of at least 40 feet. She created a brochure with a cover letter and did a mailing to the people on that list. She had a number of inquiries, had several showings and sold the property to someone on that list. That's a very targeted, cost effective, and time efficient way to market. If you can target your buyer in this way—including geographically — the chances are good you can find a relevant mailing list. (More on this in Chapter 10.)

Monitor new home inventory

In some markets there is an opportunity to list and market new homes for builders. Even if this opportunity does not exist in your community, it is important to be familiar with the new luxury home inventory. New homes are competitive with the resale homes that you list. Buyers will compare values, so it is important that you know both the competitive resale product and the new home inventory in order to price your resale listings appropriately. You will also find that sometimes a new home will be a better comparable than a resale if the new home has features and amenities that match your subject property or was built by the same builder. Knowing the market means being knowledgeable about both new and resale homes.

Use information to position yourself as an expert

Taking the time to gather information not only makes you more knowledgeable about the market and gives you information to use to inform and negotiate with buyers and sellers but also, if you are creative, can help you position yourself as an expert quickly. Here's a case in point:

A young man in the Detroit suburban area started in the residential real estate business with the goal of specializing in upper-tier waterfront properties. The first thing he did was gather information about the market. He pulled MLS data for the top 10 percent of the market and calculated the important statistics.

Since he was a decent writer, he took the statistical information that he had gathered and he wrote six short articles about what was happening in the upper price ranges along the lakeshore in suburban Detroit. He sent the six short articles to the business editor (not the real estate editor) of *The Detroit Free Press*.

Sure enough, he got a phone call from the editor indicating they'd never had such specific information about what was happening in the upper-tier lakefront property market. The editor asked permission to run the articles, one a week for the next six weeks on the front page of the Saturday business section. He told the young man he would be featured as a guest contributor with photograph and byline.

The agent's branch manager told me that the week the second article ran, the young agent's phone was already ringing with people saying, "I understand you're the expert in lake shore properties. We'd like to have you come out and talk about listing our home," or "I see that you're the expert in lake front properties. We're interested in buying. When can we talk about getting together?" This was a brand new agent doing a good job of creating the perception that he was an expert. He jump-started his business. His next very important step was to demonstrate his competence.

Chapter 5:

Targeting Rich Buyer and Rich Seller Prospects

Categories of luxury home buyers and sellers

If we define the luxury market to include $500,000 and above homes, we would include the following in our target list of prospects for luxury homes:

1. **Affluent households** with high incomes who spend most of what they earn to support an affluent lifestyle.

2. **Million Dollar Asset Households** are closely related to the group above but have accumulated significant assets even though they may not have high net worth. They are often spenders rather than savers.

3. **Atypical millionaires** who are **spending** their money (most millionaire households are savers who don't live in an upper priced property. Surprised? Read the books *The Millionaire Next Door* and *The Millionaire Mind* by Tom Stanley.)

4. Buyers of million dollar homes

5. **Inheritors** (There is a huge transfer of wealth occurring from the Depression and World War II generations to adult Baby Boomers.)

In some markets, add this market segment to the list:

6. **Wealthy immigrants** (Immigrants are more likely to become millionaires than the average American.)

29

We'll analyze each of these five target groups, but first let's look at old money, new money, and a group called ultra consumers.

Old money, new money, and the ultra consumer

When I first started training real estate agents to work in the luxury home market, somebody said to me, "Laurie you should distinguish between old money and new money consumers, because there are differences." I also decided that there is an important third category, what we might call the ultra consumers or strained affluents. These are the folks who are stretching to live as affluent a lifestyle as possible. They s-t-r-e-t-c-h to live in an expensive home, to drive an expensive a car, and to dress as well as possible.

As real estate agents we love these ultra consumers because typically they are fueling the upper tier. They come in at the entry level of the luxury home market and allow other affluent households to buy up. They also represent a large part of the luxury home market segment. If we compare them to new money and old money prospects, they probably share more of the characteristic of new money prospects.

What are the old money/new money differences? The differences listed below are generalizations, but they serve the purpose of stimulating you to ask yourself some important questions about your prospects.

Old money may be cash poor. They simply may not have access to their funds. Their money may be tied up in trusts or controlled investments.

Old money may want you to be discreet, discreet, discreet.

To illustrate, I have a friend who sells real estate in Connecticut not far from New York City. Her community is an old money market with a great many beautiful estate properties. One day she received a phone call from a homeowner who said,

"I would like you to come out and talk about listing our estate. However, we want you to know up front that we have some marketing ground rules."

She said, "I'd be delighted to market your home for you. What are the ground rules?"

They said, "First ground rule, we don't want a sign."

"That's not a problem," she answered. "In fact, in this community we're very often restricted from using signs."

They continued, "We want no mention of our home in the multiple listing system. We want no advertising. We don't want anyone in your office to know it's for sale. In fact, we don't want anybody to know it's for sale. We just want you to sell it."

Now that's a bit of a challenge. Fortunately, the agent has worked in that marketplace for more than 35 years and she knows just about everybody in her community. So, she sat down and defined the kind of buyer that she thought might want that property and be able to afford it. She thought about all the people she knew in her community and in her sphere of influence who matched her definition of a likely buyer, and she began to telephone them. She said, "IF I were able to bring onto the market a property which meets the following description, would you have an interest?" She sold the home as a result of one of those calls. This is an example of how old money sometimes wants you to be discreet to the point of almost tying your hands behind your back in terms of marketing. Don't be surprised if old money prospects want to protect their privacy.

Old money may also be conservative in the product they buy. Often they prefer a totally different kind of home with a different set of amenities than do new money prospects. They may gravitate to a traditional property while new money may lean toward something a bit flashier.

Old money may be less likely to look wealthy. Don't fall into the trap of evaluating people based on how they look. Not long ago, high tech markets had lots of dot-com millionaires. Agents in cities like Seattle, San Francisco, and Austin talked about twenty-somethings who ambled into the real estate office in shorts and flip-flops wanting to buy a house. The next thing the agents knew they were handling all cash transactions for million-dollar-plus properties. The dot-com millionaires may be less common than they were a just a few years ago, but it's still dangerous to jump to conclusions based on how prospects look. A broker in Florida is still embarrassed about instructing his assistant to tell the old guy in the overalls who came in to inquire about buying land, that the manager was out for the day. What did the "old guy" do? He drove his pickup truck to another office where an agent happily sold him the land for the first Super Wal-Mart in Florida. The less than wealthy looking client was the second richest man in America at the time—Sam Walton. Don't judge people's pocketbooks based on appearances, especially in the case of old money prospects who may not necessarily look affluent.

On the other hand, your new-money prospects are earning their money now, they have access to their funds and these **new-money clients may be all cash buyers**.

New money may be comfortable with publicity. If you sell the most expensive property ever sold in your market area, and you and your manager want to send out a press release announcing the record setting sale, your old money homebuyer may say, "Please don't!" and have palpitations of the heart just thinking about it. New money, on the other hand, may not only give you permission to contact the media, they may volunteer to stand in front of the house for the photograph.

New money may want a little more flash —a trophy house with impressive amenities. An agent in New England recently shared a story about new money buyers who purchased a home in a prestigious old money area. The neighborhood was so wooded, the agent told me, that you felt like you were driving down a country lane. Part of its charm and desirability was that you couldn't see the homes, just the gates and mailboxes.

"I was shocked," she said, "when I dropped by about six months after closing. The trees screening their home were gone.

When I asked if the trees had caught a disease and died, they said no, they had cut them down so people could see their beautiful home."

Privacy was less important than visibility. Different people have different priorities.

While these points are generalizations, they should spark your thinking about your prospects and where they stand on issues such as privacy or the desire for a trophy home. Understanding prospects' points of view and lifestyle choices can give you valuable insight into how to work with them more effectively.

1. Affluent households

While the median household income in the United States is a bit under $42,000 annually, almost a quarter of all households earn $75,000 or more. Here's how the Census Bureau breaks out income.

U.S. Household Earnings		
Earnings	**Number of Households**	**Percentage**
$100,000 - $149,999	8,315,735	7.78 %
$150,000 - $199,999	2,397,037	2.24 %
$200,000 or more	2,297,314	2.15 %
Households earning		
$100,000 plus	13,010,086	12.17 %
Source: U.S. Census Bureau, 2000 Supplementary Survey, Published June 2001		

Mendelsohn Media Research, based in New York City, has spent 25 years doing extensive research to track the spending and other habits of the top 25 percent of the nation's households as measured by income. *The 2001 Mendelsohn Affluent Head of House Survey, HHI $75,000+ & nbsp* breaks the top quartile of the nation's households into three income categories beginning at $75,000.

$75,000 to just under $100,000

$100,000 to just under $200,000

$200,000 and above

Although Mendelsohn's first income category is bit below the $100,000 and above income range we are most interested in, the study's statistics and insights—particularly as they relate to households with $1 million or more in assets—are interesting and relevant to any analysis of affluent consumers.

How do they make their money? The majority of heads of households earning $75,000 or more fall into five broad occupational categories as seen in the chart below.

Occupations of Affluent Heads of Households

(Employed heads of households earning $75,000 or more)

Professional	32 %
Management/Business/Finance	32 %
Office or Administrative Support	8 %
Sales	7 %
Technical	5 %
Other	15 %

3 out of 10 in these two categories are CEOs

Source: *2001 Mendelsohn Affluent HOH Survey*, HHI $75,000+ & nbsp
© Mendelsohn Media Research, NYC, 2001

Nationally, the affluent market is dominated by a high proportion of business owners, self-employed professionals, high tech entrepreneurs, CEOs, and other corporate executives. There are other important occupational segments. Some markets have affluent media personalities, entertainers, or sports figures. Other markets may have large concentrations of successful lawyers, doctors, or top sales people. Analyze the affluent occupational segments in your community and identify the opportunities. Identifying the occupations of the affluent allows you to target these households more effectively and to customize your marketing approach. (See the marketing ideas section for examples of how to do this.)

The highest earners are online

Numerous research studies indicate that affluent homebuyers and sellers are using the Internet in their real estate information gathering and expect their agents to be using e-mail and promoting listings online. (There's more on this later in the book.) The 2001 *Mendelsohn's Affluent Head of Household Survey, Household Income $75,000+* documents this. Of the *households earning $200,000 or more*, 95% use a computer at home, 90% have Internet access, and 57% have online access both at home and at work. Forty two percent report having three or more computers at home, 86% use e-mail to communicate, 72% gather travel information from the Web and 48% make their travel arrangements online. The Web is a financial management tool for these householders: 53% use it obtain information about financial products, 25% bank online, and 19% actually do financial securities transactions on the Internet.

Although the survey did not specifically look at the use of the Internet in real estate, the National Association of Realtors' *Profile of Home Buyers and Sellers, 2002* indicates that two thirds of those who have Internet access use the Web to shop for listings. Given the high use of the Internet by the affluent, it seems reasonable to assume that the use of the Internet to research properties is even greater among rich buyers and sellers. What's more, research from Dan Richard of The Gooder Group, a Virginia-based real estate marketing company, indicates that

74 percent of those going online to look at properties do so *before* contacting a real estate agent. This is changing the way prospects choose their real estate agents, making it more important than ever before that you have your listings online and that you respond promptly (within hours not days) to all e-mail queries from prospects.

The highest earners are active in sports

Heads of household earning $200,000 or more still find time to exercise and participate in sports. They are significantly more likely than the general population to play tennis, snow ski, sail, play golf, and go power boating. The activities most often pursued based on the average number of days the affluent heads of households participated in the activity in the past 12 months are listed below. You'll also find the affluent attending spectator sporting events.

Sport	# Of days participated
Fitness Walking	73 days
Jogging	60 days
Tennis	33 days
Golf	32 days
Swimming	28 days

Source: *2001 Mendelsohn Affluent HOH Survey, HHI $75,000+ & nbsp* © Mendelsohn Media Research, NYC, 2001

2. "Million Dollar Asset" households

The three charts that follow look at households that have accumulated at least $1 million worth of major assets. I've chosen to call these households Million Dollar Asset households to differentiate them from true millionaires.

It is important to note that Mendelsohn's Million Dollar Asset households are NOT necessarily millionaire households, since Mendelsohn's calculation is an asset-plus-income figure as opposed to a net worth calculation. The Million Dollar Asset households have at least $1 million in assets when you total the value of their home, any other real estate they own, the face value of insurance policies, stocks or other securities, and the amount of their annual income. Mortgages, debts, or other liabilities are not part of Mendelsohn's analysis. However, Mendelsohn's Million Dollar Asset household is a household with assets and an affluent lifestyle.

By contrast, in a millionaire household all the assets minus all the liabilities results in a NET figure equaling or exceeding $1 million.

The chart below takes the top quartile (actually the top 24%) of U.S. households, breaks it into three income groups, and then looks at the percentage each group represents of the total. It also takes the households in the top quartile that have at least $1 million in assets and shows which income group (as a percentage) those "Million Dollar Asset" households come from.

Analyzing the Top Quartile of U.S. Households

Income	% of Top Quartile		% of "Million Dollar Asset" Hoseholds*
$75,000 to just under $100,000	11%	⇨	27%
$100,000 to just under $200,000	44%	⇨	51%
$200,000 and above	45%	⇨	22%

Source: *2001 Mendelsohn Affluent HOH Survey, HHI $75,000+ & nbsp*
© Mendelsohn Media Research, NYC, 2001

Note the disproportionate number of high asset households that the two lower income categories represent. This would seem to imply that, on average, the highest income category is not investing as much in real estate, insurance, or stocks/bonds/securities as the two lower income groups. Perhaps the $200,000 and above income category has a higher percentage of ultra consumers?

Average Value of Principal Residence

Percent of "Million Dollar Asset" household's total assets represented by principal residence

Income	Total Asset	% Home*	Home Value
$75,000 to under $100,000	$665,100	31 %	$206,181
$100,000 to $200,000	$1033,900	26 %	$268,814
$200,000 and above	$2,422,800	20 %	$363,400

* This figure is the percentage home value represents of total assets.
Source: *2001 Mendelsohn Affluent HOH Survey, HHI $75,000+ & nbsp*
© Mendelsohn Media Research, NYC, 2001

One in four of the affluent households in Mendelsohn's study owns or rents two or more residential properties. Many have non-residential real estate investments as well. The chart below looks at the value of real estate, other than the principal residence, which these affluent households own.

Average Value of Other Real Estate

Percent of "Million Dollar Asset" household's total assets represented by real estate other than principal residence

Income	Total Assets	% other R.E.*	Value other R.E.
$75,000 to just under $100,000	$665,100	9 %	$59859
$100,000 to just under $200,000	$1,033,900	10 %	$103,390
$200,000 and above	$2,422,800	15 %	$363,420

*This figure is the percentage other real estate represents of total assets
Source: *2001 Mendelsohn Affluent HOH Survey, HHI $75,000+ & nbsp*
© Mendelsohn Media Research, NYC, 2001

What else might be useful to know about these Million Dollar Asset households that might give us networking ideas, insight about lists to rent, or other ideas for finding prospects?

18% are on a corporate board of directors

16% visited Europe in the past year

16% have country club memberships

24% own or lease a luxury car

25% purchase wine by the case

These facts suggest that lists of corporate boards might make a good target list. There are clues here as to whom you should network with—travel agents, luxury car salespeople, wine merchants, club membership directors, and owners of luxury inns.

While many of these Million Dollar Asset households may also have mortgages, car loans, credit card debt, and other liabilities that keep them from the ranks of true millionaires, they are affluent spenders, they populate the lower level of upper tier home buyers and sellers, and there are lots of them. By and large, this is an excellent prospect group for luxury homes.

3. Millionaires

Millionaire households are those whose net worth (or total assets minus liabilities) equals $1 million or more. The median household net worth in the U.S. is just under $72,000. Estimates are that there are about 3.5 million millionaire households in the United States. If you remove home equity from the net worth equation, the number probably drops to just under 3 million households.

Despite the frequent perception that the average millionaire is a high roller, the average millionaire might be characterized by three words —frugal, frugal, frugal. The average millionaire achieved his or her financial status by saving, not spending. For statistical specifics on millionaires, read Thomas Stanley's books, *The Millionaire Next Door* and *The Millionaire Mind*. (He did not allow information from his books to be quoted here.)

I recently encountered an example of the millionaire attitude in Las Vegas where I was speaking at a national convention. I asked a bellman, a young man in his early thirties, to help me move several boxes of materials into the meeting room. When he realized that the meeting was a national real estate convention, he started talking to me about his financial theories.

"You know," he said, "My wife and I bought a nice house here in Vegas with eighteen hundred square feet and a pool. We have just one child so we have plenty of room. We're making mortgage payments twice a month so we can pay off our mortgage faster. In seven more years my mortgage will be fully paid.

"I'm also a saver," he said. "I have an I.R.A and an annuity stock investment program. It's my goal to retire by age 50, move back home to Florida, buy a new house and a boat, and do nothing but play golf. My wife is saying we need to buy up and I'm saying, no honey, we need to retire at age fifty."

This young man may not be a millionaire YET. But his philosophy is consistent with the mentality that creates millionaires. Typical millionaires are savers and they spend conservatively.

Oops! The average millionaire doesn't look like the best prospect for upper tier properties. **It is the atypical millionaire we want, the one who has made money and is now spending it**.

Where will you find millionaires? As bankers or stock brokers can tell you, millionaires are most likely to be business owners and self employed professionals. Top corporate executives are also on the list. Sports stars, media personalities, and other celebrities are also likely millionaires.

Two quick suggestions for spotting millionaires who might be likely home purchasers include: watching the lists of insider/executive stock sales for publicly held companies in your market (you can find these reports online), and networking with business brokers to find successful business owners who are selling their firms and will have the proceeds to make lifestyle changes. If you can develop or purchase lists of millionaires, do market to individuals on those lists. At some point, the frugal millionaire may decide to enjoy a life style change and spend his children's inheritance.

4. Owners of million dollar homes

According to the Census Bureau only .6 percent of homeowners occupy homes worth $1 million or more. This represents 313,759 homes. What's the profile of these rich homeowners? NAR and *Unique Homes* magazine have conducted joint research on **buyers of million-dollar homes**. In general this group is younger, has a smaller family, and earns substantially more than the average millionaire. Here are some of the key findings:

Million-Dollar Buyer profile

- 47 years old
- Married with one child
- 86 % purchased through a real estate agent
- 54 % used a luxury home magazine as an information source

- 20 % bought more than 500 miles away from previous residence
- They take their time when shopping for a home! 40% looked for six months or more, 28% looked for a year.

The million dollar home prospect is more likely to use a real estate agent than the average buyer or seller. More than half of them used a luxury home magazine as a resource when looking for property. This use of magazines is important to know when you are creating your marketing plan for a million-dollar-plus listing. The fact that two out of 10 buy more than 500 miles away from their previous home emphasizes the importance of doing regional and national promotion (putting your listings on the Internet is important in this price range). Million-dollar homebuyers will also require your patience since they take their time when shopping for a home.

Since many million-dollar homebuyers are business people, expect them to apply some of the same guidelines they use in business when making home investment decisions. These guidelines will include:

- Understand current market values
- Negotiate price
- Seek out motivated sellers
- Avoid time pressures
- Recognize that there are other alternatives

When we understand that the majority of the very wealthy are business people, these rules come as no surprise. The home buying rules are probably very similar to the rules a businessperson would have for an acquisition of another firm or for the investment in a substantial business asset. However, a home purchase is an emotional process. One challenge you face when working with rich buyers is to help the buyers make what will be mostly emotional decisions while still feeling that they are honoring their intellectual, logical rules for buying.

Billionaires fit into this super-rich category. *Forbes* publishes a list of the world's billionaires each year. In 2002, William H. Gates, III held the top spot as the world's richest man with $52.8 billion. There were 243 billionaires in the U.S. in 2002, according to *Forbes*, and 254 in the remainder of the world. (See the March 18, 2002 issue of *Forbes* for details.) The publication also produces a list of the 100 highest paid entertainers and athletes in the world. (See the July 8, 2002 issue of *Forbes*.)

5. Inheritors

The United States is in the midst of a huge transfer of wealth largely driven by the fact that the generation born in the first part of the 1900s is dying and the Baby Boom generation is inheriting. A Merrill Lynch report on the transfer of wealth predicts that from 1996 to 2005 there will be 100,000 settlements of $1,000,000 or more. In addition, the report (found on their Website) says, about two million people will inherit an average of $189,000 each.

While not all these heirs will be made wealthy, many of them will take this new money and combine it with home equity or other assets and move up. Others will fund children's educations, buy second homes, invest in stocks and bonds, or acquire other assets. To identify these inheritors, develop referral relationships with trust attorneys, accountants, those who probate wills, and financial advisors.

6. Wealthy immigrants

Immigration accounts for nearly half of the population growth in the United States. Legal immigrants have been flowing into the U.S. at a rate of almost a million per year for more than two decades. Estimates are that another 300,000 come in illegally each year and remain. Immigrant households represent a high percentage of today's homebuyers and expectations are that they will represent as many as one in three of all homebuyers by 2010.

The good news for the real estate community is that although the million or so annual foreign-born arrivals to the U.S. used to move predictably to states like California, New York, Florida, and Texas, new immigration patterns began to emerge in the late 1990s. While the sheer number of new arrivals is still highest in the traditional immigrant destination states, the immigrant population is growing at a faster rate in a variety of other states spread across the country from Oregon to Virginia and from Idaho to Kansas.

The shift in the settlement pattern of new arrivals means that immigration now helps fuel many more housing markets across the U.S. For example, Hispanics and Asians are arriving in Colorado in record numbers, Asians are moving to Nebraska, and immigrants from the former Soviet Union are flowing into Texas.

These new Americans generally share the *American Dream* —homeownership is an important goal and many foreign-born households reach a high homeownership rate within less than 10 years. Many are in a position to buy even sooner. For instance, the typical Asian immigrant comes to the U.S. with more education, a larger family, and a higher income than the average American. The Mortgage Bankers Association of America estimates that immigrants already in the U.S. could create the demand for four million or more homes over the next decade or two.

Although special government programs are available to make homeownership more easily achievable for all immigrants, the groups we are interested in are those who arrive with wealth or who accumulate wealth once they are here. In fact, households of immigrants are more likely to become millionaire households than households headed by individuals born in the U.S.

The challenge for real estate brokers and agents is to tap into this large and growing segment of the market. Language and cultural differences require that real estate professionals have new resources and competencies. Many brokerage firms publish lists of agents who speak foreign languages and promote those agents online. Brokers are beginning to recruit more aggressively from their areas' foreign-born populations. Some agents are choosing to mentor and then partner with a new agent in these cultural groups. Agents are attending special training sessions focused on building cross-cultural skills. If you are targeting this growing market segment it will help to be bilingual and to understand the culture, attitudes, and manners of the group you've targeted. Build your reputation within these groups and loyalty and referrals will often follow.

One challenge with recent arrivals can be the lack of credit ratings or financial relationships. Even their assets can be an issue. What do you do with a buyer who wants to make a down payment on a home and has jewelry and gold coins rather than a checking account?

States with Fastest Growing Immigrant Populations

State	Number of foreign born 1999	1990	% Increase
Arizona	671,000	276,000	143%
Maryland	508,000	311,000	63%
Virginia	495,000	310,000	60%
N. Carolina	307,000	116,000	164%
Georgia	288,000	173,000	66%
Nevada	274,000	104,000	162%
Oregon	266,000	138,000	92%
Colorado	255,000	142,000	80%
Kansas	128,000	62,000	105%
Oklahoma	105,000	64,000	63%
Utah	93,000	57,000	62%
S. Carolina	86,000	48,000	78%
Iowa	82,000	45,000	83%

Kentucky	80,000	32,000	147%
Idaho	78,000	28,000	174%
Alabama	77,000	42,000	83%
Arkansas	67,000	25,000	165%
Nebraska	61,000	27,000	130%
Mississippi	33,000	21,000	57%

Chapter 6

Understanding Motivations of Rich Buyers and Rich Sellers

The rich are different

F. Scott Fitzgerald once said to Hemingway, "The rich are different from you and me." Hemingway's less-than-star struck response was "Yes, they have more money." But they're different in some other meaningful ways. Let's look at their motivations. They are not need-oriented. They are not buying a house to have a roof over their heads. They are interested in the ideal location, architectural excellence, quality of construction, status, the view, the neighbors, and the right package of home amenities. In short, they are looking for something special, and sometimes they approach the home buying and selling process very differently from the average client.

The wealthy can afford to be spontaneous. I was talking to a California agent who said, "Let me give you an example of spontaneous. I was working with a high-powered dual career couple who called from the east coast to introduce themselves and say they were coming to California. First thing they said to me on the phone was, 'We are so excited. All of our married life, our dream has been to live in southern California on a cliff overlooking the Pacific. We cannot wait to move. We need your help in finding just the right lot, just the right builder, and we want to build our dream home.'"

"I said, 'No problem, I can help you with that.' They came, I helped them. Eighteen months later it was time for the property to close. I sat down with them as they were finalizing the paperwork and said, "Well what's the plan, when will the moving trucks arrive?"

The husband said, "Well, we need to talk to you about that. When we finish here we'd like to sit down with you and list this house."

"After this couple had gone through eighteen months of building their dream home together what do you think my first thought was?"

"Yes!"

My second thought was that they were getting a divorce. So, I somewhat tentatively said, "I'll be delighted to list the house for you, but why have you decided to sell?" I was expecting them to say "divorce."

"Instead they said, 'After going through the eighteen month process of building this house, now we know what we *really* want in our dream home. This house was a great dry run. We want you to find another lot for us. We love our builder, we'll stick with him, but now we are ready to build our dream property. We're going to sell this one.' This is certainly more spontaneous than the typical prospect can afford to be."

Upper-tier buyers and sellers can afford to be fickle. An agent who works in the Atlanta market was called to list a well-known estate in Buckhead, a prestigious and expensive part of town. This was a very high profile property owned by an international couple. The agent made the appointment and toured the home. She felt the house was in perfect condition. Every blade of grass in the yard looked hand trimmed. This house needed nothing. Right off the bat the seller said, "We want to sell this house as is."

The agent said, "This house certainly needs no cosmetic work."

The seller said, "No, no, you don't understand, we want to sell as is —with the Oriental rugs and the antiques in the rooms, the art on the walls, the pots and pans in the kitchen. We just want to take some of our personal possessions and leave."

If you're selling a resort condo or a wealthy individual's third or fourth home, it may not be too unusual to sell it fully furnished. In the middle of Buckhead in Atlanta, it is unusual. In old money Buckhead, chances are the buyers are going to have their own things. This situation requires a fairly complex market analysis because you're going to have to call in experts to price things other than the property. And if the buyer doesn't want all the furnishings and other contents of the home, then you may have to help coordinate the auctioning or other disposal of the contents. A fickle seller or buyer can create complexity.

Despite the story above, and to further illustrate the fickleness of the wealthy buyer, it has not been uncommon in cities with dot-com millionaires for young buyers who are busy or perhaps not yet confident about their taste to want to buy a fully furnished home. One good example of this occurred in Newport Coast, Calif. Pacific Design Estates, a high-end builder, created a 7,500 square foot Mediterranean design home with all the modern features and the ambiance of a Venetian palazzo. The home sold fully furnished for $8.8 million cash in five days.

Wealthy sellers and buyers can be on a different time schedule than your average buyer or seller. I was visiting an Arizona health spa one January and got up one morning to do an early morning walk through the desert. The path would accommodate two people side by side. There were probably thirty people doing this walk and everybody was bunched together in pairs. There were two ladies side by side in front of me talking about real estate. It was an interesting conversation and I have no shame, so I paced myself and listened. The conversation went something like this. One was saying to the other, "We've decided to sell the estate on Long Island and my real estate agent is pushing me to put it on the market now, in January. I really think I'd prefer to list in the spring when the gardens look fabulous, but my agent keeps harping on January."

The seller's idea to wait might have struck me as reasonable had I not just had a conversation with a broker from Long Island. I had asked, "How's business?"

He answered, "Business is wonderful."

"In January?" His answer wasn't what I had expected.

He said, "Laurie, in the upper tier on Long Island in the markets that I serve, January is the hottest month of the year. Don't you know what happens the end of December and first part of January in New York City?"

I shook my head no.

"The Wall Street bonuses are paid. The Wall Streeters are flush with cash and many want to move up. Long Island is an easy commute to the tip of Wall Street and we have wonderful estate properties. Thanks to Wall Street, January is my office's busiest month in the higher price ranges."

January is not the busiest month in other prices ranges on Long Island. The upper tier is on a different schedule from the rest of the market. Be sure that you are aware of anything that might create different peak periods for the high price ranges in your area.

How the rich choose real estate agents

NAR/*Unique Homes* magazine research reveals these insights about rich buyers and sellers and their criteria for selecting an agent:

- The affluent want an agent who knows the market (This can be further defined as knowing both the luxury market niche **and** the geographic market area)

- If they've used an agent before and have been happy with the agent's service, they are inclined to consider using the agent again

- The quality of the listing presentation is very important—a better listing presentation can override a previous relationship

- Affluent prospects say that offering a special luxury home marketing system will give you a marketing edge, especially if it includes a strong print advertising plan. Examples of luxury home marketing systems would include Coldwell Banker Previews,™ RE/MAX Renowned Properties,™ Century 21 Fine Homes and Estates,™ GMAC Elegant Homes,™ and ERA International Properties.™ Marketing assistance is also offered through special organizations including Christies, Sotheby, and Who's Who in Luxury Home Marketing. Some local and regional brokerages have their own luxury home marketing programs. If your firm doesn't have a marketing system, develop your own special program for expensive properties.

Many affluent sellers are business owners, self-employed professionals, and corporate executives. These are bottom-line oriented individuals who will evaluate you based on how they perceive your ability to get the job done. In short, you must convince them that you have the skills necessary to sell the house in the time period they require, for the best price, with the least inconvenience to them.

Do you have to live the affluent lifestyle to capture upper-end business? No. But you do have to create visibility in the niche you are targeting with a focus on positioning and promoting yourself as a luxury home expert. Then, you must deliver on that promise and provide expert service.

Chapter 7

Evaluating your Competition

Analyze your competition

To determine with whom you are competing in the luxury home market, pull sales and listings in the top price ranges and look to see which brokerage firms and agents are most active. This will give you a clear picture of who is targeting this market and the market share controlled by each competitor.

Just identifying the competition isn't enough. It is also important to have a sense of what your competition is offering. Do they have a special program for luxury homes? Do they create full color brochures? Produce a special luxury magazine? Do they have a national network to use as a resource? Try to determine their strengths and weaknesses—then you can determine how best to compete. This process will also help you determine with whom you need to be networking.

The competitive analysis form below is an organized way to evaluate other brokers who compete in upper tier. You will be competing for prospects with these firms and their agents so it is important to know their strengths and weaknesses.

Competitive Analysis

Competitor	Affiliation

Profile: # Agents   Transactions ⌐ Top 10% of Market ⌐   Share ⌐ Top 10% of market ⌐ %

Offices $ Volume   Up/Down?

Agent Profile:

Three words which describe company

COMPETITIVE ANALYSIS

STRENGTHS	WEAKNESSES

Strategy they appear to be implementing?_____

Other Comments:_____

In doing your analysis, look at the number of transaction sides (listings or sales) and the total dollar volume of business your competitor did in the last 12 months in the top 10 percent of the market. Calculate what percentage of the upper tier this represents. That percentage will be their market share in the upper tier. Is this market share trending up or decreasing? What do you perceive to be the strengths of their marketing efforts for luxury homes? Where might they be weak and vulnerable? A close review of the form will give you additional insight into analyzing the competition so you can structure your efforts to out-think and out-market them.

Chapter 8

Recognizing the Characteristics for Success

Understanding that YOU are your product

You are in the business of listing and selling real estate, but before you can sell a home to a buyer, you must first convince the buyer that you are the agent who can best help with his or her home finding. You must sell yourself, your capabilities, your experience, and your skills. Before you can market and sell a listing, you must convince the seller that you are the agent who can best market the property. Again, you must sell yourself. In real estate, the first sale you must make is YOU. Thus, it follows that you are your product and that **you need to package, position, and promote yourself just like a product** in order to be successful in the residential real estate business.

Packaging yourself includes projecting professionalism with the way you dress. It means having a firm handshake, looking people in the eye, and carrying yourself with confidence.

Positioning yourself is also important to your success. The positioning or perception that you want to create in peoples' minds is that you as a real estate sales associate are unique and better able to meet the needs of the affluent buyer and seller. Simply stated, that should be the goal of your marketing. Then, you must deliver on that promise. You must, in fact, be unique and better able to meet their needs.

Promoting can be defined as your marketing —how you create and communicate the perception of uniqueness for yourself and how you advertise and market your services and your listings (more on this in subsequent chapters).

Characteristics for success in the luxury niche

When I first began working in the luxury home market, I went to my broker and asked what advice she could give me about working in the luxury home niche. She told me that the *process* of buying and selling expensive homes doesn't really differ much from the average transaction. What is different, she told me, is that the luxury home niche is a more sophisticated market and it demands a higher level of communication and professionalism—and some special characteristics. Here are the five characteristics she suggested I'd need to succeed, plus two others.

1. Look and act successful

In Dallas, where I live, there is a well-known broker who had a boutique luxury home company (she has since sold it). When she trained her new agents she'd tell them "fake it until you make it." Initially that made me a little bit uncomfortable. Then I realized what she was really saying. From your first day in the luxury market, you must project confidence and competence. I think she's right. One characteristic you must have is the ability to project confidence and competence.

2. Demonstrate professionalism and competence

The second characteristic is to deliver on that implicit promise by demonstrating your professionalism and competence. Projecting the right image is important, but you must also have the necessary skills.

3. Be unintimidated by money, power, and fame

Success characteristic number three is to be unintimidated by money, power or fame (or at least not so intimidated that you can't function). Working in the high price ranges often puts you in touch with celebrities, well-known business executives, sports stars, the fabulously rich, and other people who are high profile. An agent who is overawed or intimidated is not going to perform at peak levels.

4. Be memorable—do business with style

(But you don't have to live a wealthy lifestyle)

You will also benefit from doing business with a little bit of style or flair. Standing out from the crowd in a positive way is good marketing. Create something that makes you memorable in the marketplace. Some agents dress with unusual flair, others drive cars that stand out on the road, other agents adopt visual or verbal hooks.

In metro Seattle, an agent who specializes in luxury waterfront properties always has his listings photographed from the water with a small yellow rubber ducky floating in one corner of the photograph. His listings are immediately identifiable and they catch attention and get a second look. You may forget his name, but you won't forget the rubber ducky. An agent in the San Francisco Bay area has a gift box delivered to prospects before a listing presentation. Inside, sellers find a brief video about the agent's special marketing program for luxury homes, plus popcorn, cold drinks, and a note to enjoy the movie.

These are examples of fun ideas that are consistent with particular agents' style and help make them memorable. By all means implement ideas like these, but also remember that offering exceptional service is the best way to stand out.

Often when I speak to agents who aspire to work in the luxury home market they ask if one has to live in a million dollar house or drive a Mercedes to work with the affluent. The answer is absolutely not. While it helps to be memorable, it is not necessary to live a rich and famous lifestyle to work with that market segment.

One of my favorite real estate stories involves an agent from New Jersey. This young man told me that when he first decided to work in the upper tier he was really intimidated. He wasn't intimidated by the wealthy buyers and sellers that he knew he'd be working with. Instead, he was intimidated by other already successful luxury home agents. He was concerned about how well he could compete and the fact that he didn't have an affluent image.

After some aggressive prospecting, he generated an opportunity to do a listing presentation on a wonderful country estate. He learned that he was the fourth and last presenter in the line-up. He did his homework to find out who his competitors for the listing would be. He knew the first agent would show up in her shiny new Mercedes. The second agent drove a nice BMW. The third agent had a car and driver. He told me he was totally intimidated by what he perceived to be their obvious success. He, on the other hand, would have to show up in his old —but clean and serviceable —Volvo.

The day of his listing presentation came. He drove down the private lane with its canopy of trees to the estate. Arriving at the house, he pulled into the huge stone drive in front of the house and pulled his old Volvo over as far as possible to one side. Then he climbed the steps to the big, hand-carved double wooden doors with a huge brass knocker. He rapped on the door, and, sure enough, the owner himself opened the doors. The young agent said he stood there with his heart in his throat as he watched the owner's eyes go from him to the Volvo, back to him, back to the Volvo, and finally back to him. The agent stood there for what seemed like forever before the owner said, "Well, at last, a down-to-business automobile." At that moment, the agent said, he knew that the listing was his. Sure enough, he got the listing and the opportunity to demonstrate his competence. He also recognized that you don't have to live a wealthy lifestyle to work in the upper-tier market.

5. Use quality marketing materials

Slapdash materials, poor photocopies, and bad photographs have no place in luxury home marketing. Your materials should reflect the quality of the home you are marketing and the quality service you provide.

6. Network with other upper-tier agents

It is important to remember that the other agents who work in the luxury market can be a tremendous resource to you. You should be networking with them. Here's an example of how one group of top agents with different firms are working together to generate more business for everyone:

As movie goers in the affluent areas of North Dallas (and the fast growing Dallas suburban market of Plano) settle into their seats before the main feature film, an ad for the *Elite 20* pops on the screen inviting consumers to turn to 20 of the area's top real estate agents for help with home buying and selling.

What's especially interesting about this group of 20 of the Dallas market's top agents is that they are high powered producers from five different real estate companies—both franchised and unaffiliated firms. Current members of the group have a combined career sales volume of $3.3 billion dollars. Despite working in different brokerage firms, the agents have come together to form a working team.

These top producers have not only formed an information-sharing networking group that crosses company lines, they do joint advertising and marketing. Their advertising campaign theme is "Wouldn't you prefer a team of 20 to the power of one?" The 20 agents have a shared *Elite 20* web page; advertise together in the movies and on area billboards, and have a close working relationship.

Joy Nees, a top-performing agent, created the concept for the group in 1990. "Rather than joining a general networking group, I thought, 'Why not start a real estate networking group?' Some people said, 'Those are your competitors,' I said, 'No, they are my peers and we can help each other.'"

Each month, the members choose eight of their listings, the group tours those properties, and each agent then provides written feedback on the listings viewed. This close networking not only provides valuable feedback to the seller, the sharing often results in one *Elite 20* member listing a home and another selling it—the groups' equivalent of an in-house sale.

After the monthly tour, Nees says the group has lunch at a local country club and talks about the market, their listings, and the needs of their buyers. Between monthly meetings, Nees coordinates an "All Call" communication among members. A new listing generates a call that goes out to the other members. "Often we'll sell a property before it shows up in MLS. One member listed a contemporary on a creek lot, I dashed over that same morning with my buyer and sold the house —an example of how our buyers and sellers benefit from the group."

The agents also share resources. Nees explains, "Mold is now an issue. If I'm looking for a good, responsible inspector for a mold inspection, I place a call and get a couple of names almost immediately from the other agents."

The secret to the success of the group, according to Nees, is that the team members are what she calls "the heavy hitters" and as the group's ads say, you call on just one for the power of 20. Members of the group agree that not only do consumers benefit but the power of networking helps make the agents more successful, too.

Networking in more traditional ways also works. Hawaiian real estate agent Doug Shanefield was holding an open house when he met a man whose mother in New Jersey was in the market for an oceanfront home in Hawaii.

After a number of conversations about the prospect's requirements, Doug flew to New Jersey to present photographs and descriptions of a property he thought was a match for her desires. He even told her that he swam out to sea to check the view of the property from the water. Impressed with Shanefield and the home, the woman bought the house sight unseen.

Ten months later, the buyer called Shanefield asking if he could assist her with the sale of a cottage on Nantucket. A good networker, Shanefield quickly referred her to another agent specializing in luxury homes in Nantucket. The one bedroom cottage —which happened to be on 65 acres —sold for $19.5 million.

7. Always be ethical

This is true regardless of price range, but it is too important to go unsaid. No matter how smart or clever or informed you are, if your word cannot be trusted or you act outside the best interests of those to whom you have a fiduciary responsibility, you will not be successful in the long term. Doing what is right should be one of your business principles. Recognize that integrity, authenticity, and trust are three principals which form the foundation of success.

Chapter 9

Differentiating: Positioning Yourself as Unique and Better

In order to be unique and better able to meet the needs of rich buyers and sellers, you need to develop some special competencies.

Recognize architectural styles and terminology

Learn architectural styles and terminology. Your credibility suffers when you visit a potential listing or show a home and have no clue what architectural style or combination of styles the property is. There are numerous books available that can serve as quick references on architectural design. Go online or to the architectural section in your local bookstore and you'll find publications that will give you an overview of architectural styles.

Two book suggestions are *What Style Is It: A Guide to American Architecture* by Poppeliers, Chambers, and Schwartz (published by John Wiley & Sons) or *A Field Guide to American Houses* by Virginia and Lee McAlester (published by Alfred A. Knopf). Both books are full of sketches and photographs illustrating specific styles. If you are still learning your architectural styles, you can drive up in front of a property, flip through the book, and in fairly short order figure out what style—or as is sometimes the case, which combination of styles—a property may be. Then, you can go in to visit with the seller with at least a bit of architectural knowledge.

Use the book as you preview properties; then, when you show them, you are prepared to talk about the architecture. After you've done this for six months, you'll find that the information has transferred itself from the book into your brain and you are becoming more knowledgeable about architectural styles.

The National Trust for Historic Preservation is also an excellent resource for learning more about home design. Their informative courses on architectural styles are open to real estate agents. See Chapter 15 of this book for more information on the National Trust.

Research leading architects—Who designed a home can influence value

Research your area's leading architects, both past and present. I know you are a busy real estate agent juggling lots of things, but knowing which current architects are known for their residential designs and which architects are significant historically is very important for a variety of reasons. Who designed a home can have an impact on its value and even influence how you market it. Let me give you an illustration.

Working in Florida, particularly in the Palm Beach area, between World War I and World War II, there was an architect by the name of Addison Meisner. Meisner designed and built numerous properties for wealthy industrialists and was considered to be the premier architect in the United States in his time. He designed a fabulous house in Palm Beach for the owner and founder of the National Tea Company. As the story goes, when Meisner and the founder of the National Tea Company went to the property to do the final walk-through, they realized that the house had no staircase to the second floor. Obviously Meisner had to think fast to recover his credibility with his client. He proposed that that they add a fabulous turret containing a spiral staircase, which is what they did.

A few years ago, this property came on the market again. Imagine that you were one of the real estate agents competing for that listing. You sat down with the seller and said, "Thank you so much for the opportunity to talk to you about marketing your home. You know, this house has always fascinated me ever since I read the story about Meisner and the missing staircase." What just happened to your credibility? Do you also have a marketing hook? Could you build an entire promotional campaign for that house around the concept of the Meisner house with the missing staircase? It seems to me that you could really have some fun with that theme, get some free media exposure and generate a lot of "word of mouth" about that home. Does the fact that the house is a Meisner- designed home add value? Absolutely. The fact that it is the house with the missing staircase may even add some extra value.

In some cases, prospects who wish to build custom homes or plan to redo the home they are purchasing may ask you to suggest architects to assist them.

To familiarize yourself with *current* architects and begin to develop a resource list:

- Most metro areas have local chapters of the American Institute of Architects. You can network with this group.
- As you get to know the luxury homebuilders in your market, ask them with which architects they most commonly work.
- Watch your local newspaper and city magazines for features on luxury homes. Note the architects.
- Always ask sellers, "Do you know who designed your home?"
- If you live in a large city, watch national publications like *Architectural Digest* for features on homes in your market. The architect and interior designers will almost always be credited.

To familiarize yourself with *historic* architects:

- Visit the library and/or local historic society and ask for information on well-known local architects from the past. The local chamber of commerce is also a good resource, and many towns now have a city planning department that specializes in historic preservation.

- Watch luxury home MLS listing information for references to specific architects from the past. Then, look them up at the library or online.

Delve into your area's history

Take the time to check out a book from your local library, skim it, and learn a bit about your community's history. This will give you some great ideas for creative marketing or what I call romancing your listing. Sometimes even knowing more about your area's history than your competitors know will help you win a listing. At least, that's what a Maryland agent discovered when she went on a listing presentation in the oldest part of a community called Chevy Chase:

Chevy Chase, Maryland, is located in suburban Washington, D.C., inside the beltway. It is one of Washington's more desirable, close-in suburbs; however, when Chevy Chase was developed at the turn of the century it was not in easy commuting range. In fact, it was considered so far away that the developers positioned it as a weekend or summer community. Realizing that they needed to be creative to sell their development, the first thing they did was put in a pretty little man-made lake. They added a park area with places to picnic, a gazebo, and bandstand. They then developed their building lots. The important additional investment was a little electric trolley that ran from Chevy Chase into Washington, D.C. Then they began to promote their development to the affluent households in Washington. They said, "Come on up to Chevy Chase. Bring the family. You can picnic around the lake and use the paddleboats. When the sun begins to go down, we'll have a concert in the bandstand, you can dance on the dance floor, and we'll have fireworks over the lake. Of course, while you're there, let us show you our lots." Sounds like the pitch for a land development today, doesn't it?

Over time, they sold the lots in Chevy Chase. This was around the turn of the twentieth century, so a lot of wonderful sprawling Victorian houses with big porches were built in Chevy Chase. A couple of years ago, one of those original houses went on the market. One of the agents who had an opportunity to go out and do a listing presentation on this home met with the sellers and said, "I am just delighted to have the opportunity to talk to you about listing your home. This is one of my favorite houses in Chevy Chase. I've always admired the big wraparound porch. In fact, this is one of the very first houses built on the lake."

The sellers looked at her and said, "Wait a minute, what lake?" The lake is no longer there; it's gone. The property became so valuable that at some point along the way it was filled in and built over. The agent said, "Don't you know the history of Chevy Chase?" And the sellers said, "No, we just moved here with the last administration, and we don't know much about this area."

So, the agent told them the story about the development of Chevy Chase. They said, "Anyone who knows that much about this area is the person we want listing our home. You've got the listing." Certainly, the agent has some marketing hooks for romancing that property. It may seem like a small thing, but the more you know about your area's history, the more likely you are to find some interesting and effective ways to promote listings.

Develop your knowledge of upper-tier builders and developers

In some markets there is an opportunity to work with residential developers and new homebuilders by representing them in the marketing of building lots and homes. Even if builders will not list with you, if you are just getting started in the upper tier, it may be worth your time to volunteer to hold a new home open for a custom builder or advertise a builder's listings in order to attract prospective high-ticket buyers.

Getting to know the custom homebuilders in your market may also create opportunities for referral business. If one of their homebuyers has a home to sell, ask the builder to refer the listing to you.

Another important reason to be familiar with upper priced new home inventory is that new homes compete with resale listings. Many buyers look at both. You need to preview the properties, both new and resale, which are competitive with your listings. You need to be able to talk intelligently to the buyer who is considering a new home and be prepared show them the best available properties for their needs.

Comparables can sometimes be difficult to find when you are dealing with an expensive custom home. Turning to the new home market will sometimes give you the best comparables based on amenities, size, or other factors.

Recognize amenities that add value

According to the National Association of Homebuilders research report, *What 21st Century Homebuyers Want* (completed in 2001), buyers of $350,000 new homes want 3000 square feet, four or more bedrooms, three or more baths, and three-car garages. Kitchens with island work areas and hard surface counter tops such as Corian and granite are on the list along with high ceilings, crown moldings, French doors, skylights, and central vacuum systems. Special room requirements include sunrooms, media rooms, and home offices. Porches/decks/patios and security systems also rank high on the list of desirable or required features.

It is safe to assume these features are usually expected by the luxury homebuyer above $350,000. But the luxury buyer wants more and can afford the features that *support their lifestyles*. Gourmets and those who entertain may want professional gas ranges, large temperature-controlled wine closets, furniture-quality kitchen cabinets, and large butler's pantries for storing china, crystal, serving pieces, and flatware. Wealthy households with full staff may want kitchens that are separate from the family living area or even multiple kitchens (including a mini-kitchen in the master bedroom). Fully equipped outdoor kitchens with grilling areas are gaining popularity in warmer climates, and catering kitchens are often on the must-have list for those who entertain large groups.

Popular luxury bathroom features include heated floors, steam showers, saunas, whirlpool tubs, and sitting room/dressing room areas as well as spa/massage areas. Special purpose closets for furs, ball gowns, or luggage may be positive features. Home gyms, resistance lap-pools, tennis courts, and putting greens may be desired by those who can afford them. Home theatres are increasingly common, and built-in plasma-screen TVs are showing up in media rooms. Sometimes entire homes are wired with sophisticated music systems. Maid/staff quarters, guesthouses, and pool cabanas may also be on some buyers' must-have lists.

Many buyers have strong preferences in architectural style. Gardens may be a significant amenity for some buyers. Being able to enjoy a view of water, mountains, or a city skyline may also be important. Security systems and safe rooms may also be desired. One of the most creative luxury features I've encountered recently is the use of warming drawers (usually a kitchen amenity for keeping food hot) used in the bathroom for keeping towels toasty warm and ready to use

Construction and finish-out features that are gaining in popularity include window glass with anti-dirt glaze, European-built working windows with solid metal hardware, single-family home elevators, solar panel roofing that looks like slate, heated floors, and special ceiling treatments ranging from coffered to Trompe l'oeil painted ceilings.

There is not one list of key features for luxury homebuyers—remember these are the people who can afford a home that is customized for the way they live, work, and entertain. What is important is quality and luxury. Also recognize that certain construction materials, brands of appliances and fixtures may be selling points and may make a difference in pricing.

Ask your buyer prospects what special features are essential and what other features are desirable to them. The more you know about their lifestyle, the easier it will be to find just the right home for them. Also remember to ask your sellers what features they've most enjoyed about the home they are selling. Chances are these may be some of the key features the new buyer will be excited about as well.

Pay attention to interior design and landscape design

You don't need to be an expert in interior design and land-scape design, but you do need to know when they add value to a property or make the property desirable for a particular market segment.

An agent in the Carolinas told me that she listed a property with one of about 50 antique camellia gardens in the world. She said, "I didn't even know what a camellia looked like until I listed the house, but I knew that for some small segment of the market that garden was going to add value." She worked with the owner to develop a strategy to reach the international gardening community. She sold the house to someone who paid a premium and for whom the garden was probably more important than the home. To that buyer, the value was in the garden. Knowing that these things can matter and asking the right questions so that you can take advantage of special opportunities will help separate you from competitors.

To keep current on trends in decor and landscaping and to monitor what new amenities and features luxury homeowners desire, periodically scan publications such as *Sales and Marketing Ideas* (a bi-monthly publication of the National Sales and Marketing Council of the National Association of Home Builders) and *Architectural Digest*.

Learn to handle the multi-level sale

Often in the higher price ranges you will encounter players other than the buyer and seller. **You may work with an implementer, a screener, and invariably (but not unique to the upper tier) the ubiquitous deal killer**. Let's look at each of these roles.

The implementer supervises the service. An example of this would be a trustee. Assume a property goes into trust and it becomes the trustee's responsibility to get that property sold. The trustee is not the owner. He or she simply has the task of initiating and managing the service that you're going to provide. In some cases the implementer may be given responsibility for negotiating the deal. In other cases, an implementer is simply responsible for selecting an agent, getting the property listed, and turning the contract over to someone else to negotiate. An implementer has no emotional attachment to the property. Implementers are judged on bottom line performance. How quickly was the property sold, for how much money, and were the proceeds distributed as they were suppose to be, based on the terms and conditions of the trust? As a result they will look to you to get results. Generally you will know when you are dealing with an implementer

I did a luxury home marketing program several years ago in the Cayman Islands and the agents attending explained to me that they frequently work with implementers. Often representatives of wealthy individuals will come to the islands to buy and sell residential real estate for their clients or employers. The owners may never see the property because they're not buying it to live in, they're buying it because of tax shelter needs or other financial considerations. In these situations, the implementer selected the property and negotiated the transaction. So, depending upon where you are and what kind of a market you are in, you may interact with an implementer.

The screener is another player working with a different agenda. **The screener is usually brought into a transaction by a high profile buyer to maintain confidentiality**. Many markets have well known business people, sports stars, or celebrities from the media, entertainment, or music fields. These individuals are often at a disadvantage when negotiating to buy a residential property. If Bill Gates or Julia Roberts want to buy your home, how willing are you going to be to negotiate price? You're likely to assume the attitude that they can afford to pay full price.

The screener may be a business manager, relative, or other trusted individual who is given a description of the desired property or a list of criteria. The screener is asked to screen agents, select one or more with whom to work, and then screen properties. The screener narrows the property alternatives to just a few and the potential buyer then looks at those homes (at least hoping to remain unrecognized) and makes the selection. At this point, the screener may become an implementer or hand off the negotiation of the transaction to another representative of the celebrity.

Unless you are prequalifying prospects at first contact, you may not always realize that you are working with a screener. If you suspect that someone is a screener, ask. It is not necessary to know for whom they are screening, but it will often explain why the showing and decision process may seem to be proceeding differently. Recognize that when you're working with screeners, they have veto power. First, they're screening to find the right agent and they can choose you or not. They also have veto power over the properties. Their motivation is three-fold: finding an agent with whom both screener and principal will feel comfortable, finding homes that match the selection criteria, and, of course, maintaining confidentiality.

An agent specializing in country property in South Carolina was working with a buyer prospect and after several property showings decided that the man was screening for someone. Rapport was good and when the agent asked, the gentleman confided, on condition of confidentiality, that he was screening for a well-known singer. Several days later they looked at a property that was listed by a competing broker who was present for the showing. Something the screener said alerted the listing broker to the fact that the screener was looking for this celebrity. Later that week, the other broker ran an ad in the local newspaper that identified the celebrity by saying even so-and-so looks at our listings. The screener called his agent to say, "You've been great and you've shown me some properties which were real possibilities, but confidentiality has been breached along with her ability to negotiate. In fact, she said not only are we not going to buy in South Carolina, she told me not to waste my time looking in North Carolina." Confidentially is key when dealing with celebrities directly or with their screeners.

Another frequent player in the luxury market is the deal killer. This player often pops up in the negotiation stage. One obvious deal killer is the attorney, but others can play the role as well. A number of years ago there was an article in a national publication about business managers for the affluent. One of the business managers interviewed described a situation involving one of his clients who is a high profile actress. It seems she had found a house that she just absolutely had to have. It was listed for more than $1 million. She contracted for it. When the business manager discovered this, he stepped in and renegotiated the contract. In this case he didn't kill the transaction, but he did change it substantially. Deal killers are generally motivated by wanting to improve the deal. And, as was the case with the business manager, they are often not present at the beginning of the transaction; they are invited in or interject themselves later in the process.

Probably the most common deal killers real estate agents encounter are not in the upper tier, they are in the first time homebuyer market —mom and dad. Parents frequently interject themselves into their children's transactions. They want to be certain the kids are getting a good buy. To understand the concept of the deal killer, just think about mom and dad and the first time homebuyer, and you'll get the picture.

When the deal killer shows up, just be prepared to make the sale for a second time, explaining the benefits and educating the new player on the realities of the market.

Refine your valuation skills

Your ability to peg the price at which a unique custom home will sell is important to your credibility and success. Pricing upper end homes properly is more difficult than pricing less expensive homes for which there are many comparables. You will be concerned with size, condition, amenities, functionality, location, market activity —the same things you look at when pricing any property; but even very experienced agents can sometimes find valuing unique custom homes challenging.

An agent in the Southwest faced with pricing a custom-built 45,000-square-foot home with in- and outdoor pools, guest house, staff quarters, and an amazing list of other features actually went outside her market area to find comparably sized properties and then adjusted for market price differences as well as for other features. Even looking in other markets, the number of 45,000-square-foot homes is limited.

A number of years ago, when the market was in a severe down cycle in parts of New England, it was not uncommon for an agent preparing a market analysis on a luxury home to use the subject property as its own comparable. The agent would look at the last time the property sold, calculate how much the market prices had changed in that price range (in this case the change was a decline) and then apply that percentage to adjust the previous sales price to a current value. Going out of the area and using the subject property as its own comparable are extreme techniques but are sometimes necessary in the luxury market.

Nor is it uncommon for a prelisting appraisal to be part of the pricing process. This appraisal can be especially important when an agent feels the seller may have unrealistic expectations about price.

Occasionally in the upper tier you'll come across a home with a feature that is so unique that it is difficult to price, or so unusual it may impair your ability to sell the home, in which case it becomes a price-reducing feature. One day during the break at a training session for luxury home agents in Los Angeles, an agent told me he was in the process of listing a home but was in a bit of a quandary about pricing and salability. His concern centered around one of the home's features—an underground shooting range. He felt that for most prospects it would be a negative. He joked about doing some target marketing with licensed gun owners, but admitted that he didn't think that was the best approach. As he described the shooting range to me, I realized that it was basically just a big soundproof room with sliding targets (and probably some holes in the wall).

As we talked, it dawned on both of us that the shooting range could easily be transformed into a feature that would add tremendous value to a home in Los Angles. You have probably already guessed what we came up with. The big empty, soundproof room with targets removed could easily be marketed as a recording studio. He took a lemon of a feature and made lemon meringue pie.

No matter how effective you are at pricing property, you will invariably encounter the seller who laments, "My house must be worth more!"

A number of agents have told me that, when they encounter this objection, they ask the sellers, "If you were going to buy your home today, what would you pay for it?" Then, they tell them what the monthly payment and qualifying income would be at that price. Sellers will often say, "Oh my gosh, I had no idea," especially if they've been in their house for a while. This opens the door to explaining how too a high price will limit the number of potential buyers and lengthen the marketing time.

If you've got a seller who still insists their house is worth more, and you've negotiated, and you've looked at the statistics and you just can't get together on price, try the *Buyer for the Afternoon* approach. This doesn't work every time, but it's worth a try as a way to give your seller a dose of market reality. The script below works well with business owners, corporate executives, and self-employed professionals. Just tweak it to match your seller's situation.

Develop a script that creates a dialogue along these lines, "You're in business. Let me ask you a question. In your business, would you ever bring a new product or service into the marketplace without doing some research on how your competitors are pricing similar products or services?"

The usual response is, "Of course not."

"Well let me ask you a question. Isn't your house one of the most important products that you're going to sell this year?"

"That's right".

"So, since we're not in agreement as to the price and since your home is a very important product, I'm going to propose that we do some price comparison just like you do in your own business. I know you're busy, but since pricing your home correctly is of critical importance, I think we need to invest a few hours in pricing research. I'd like for us to go out and look at a couple of properties in the price range where you think your house should be listed and a couple of properties in the price range where I think your house should be listed. Then, we'll sit down again and talk price. Is that reasonable?"

Usually your seller will agree.

Take your seller to look at two cream of the crop, absolutely best properties in the price range where they want to list — which obviously is higher than the price range where you want to list. Then look at the two best cream puff properties in the price range where you think the home should be listed. Make sure you have previewed these properties and select carefully. This dose of market reality should help you in your negotiation of a reasonable list price.

To implement this technique, you must be knowledgeable enough about competing properties to be able to select the best properties to look at with your seller. This emphasizes the importance of previewing the entire inventory. It also puts you in the position of asking to show a listing to someone who may not be a valid prospect. Here's a situation where networking with other luxury home agents pays off. Explain to the listing agent that you are doing pricing research with a client and that you would like to preview (as opposed to show) the home and will bring your client with you. Indicate that you will be happy to provide written feedback from your perspective and share your client's comments if they would be useful to the lister in working with his or her seller. Also volunteer to reciprocate when the other agent would like to do something similar. A good agent will usually see value in this and be able to schedule an appointment for you.

Having an appraisal done up front is also a common technique for zeroing in on a listing price that you and the seller can agree upon.

Be an information source for the affluent

As your reputation as a pricing expert in the luxury home market grows, you may get a call from an owner who says, "You've been referred to me as a luxury home expert. I am not selling my house, I am taking out a loan for my business and my banker is requiring personally liability. I am working with my accountant to prepare information on my personal assets and I need a market valuation for my home. Can you help me?" Your answer should be affirmative because this is an opportunity for possible future business or to ask for a referral.

Agents who have worked for a while in the upper-tier market will usually develop extensive resource lists. Particularly those who are new to the area will ask about sources for services including (but not limited to):

- ✓ Jumbo mortgage loans
- ✓ Interior decorators
- ✓ Painters, carpet cleaners, and others who do home maintenance
- ✓ Antique and oriental rug dealers
- ✓ Craftspeople who do stonework, faux finishes, or hand-scraped inlaid hardwood floors
- ✓ Landscape designers, pool companies, or deck designers

✓ Caterers, party planners, personal chefs, and gourmet food sources

✓ Private airports with hangers for housing planes

✓ Marinas

✓ Housecleaning, pool, and plant care services

✓ Nanny finders or daycare services

✓ Personal trainers, massage therapists, hairstylists, day spas, or exercise facilities

In short, your affluent clients will often turn to you for a long list of resource recommendations. Develop contacts in all of these areas and network with them. The painter who is redoing a home before it goes on the market can be a source of referrals; the marina owner who is helping a client sell a boat before relocating can give you a tip and recommendation that leads to a listing. Interact with others who work with the wealthy. It will pay off.

Serving as a source of information is also an aspect of providing exceptional service. Some brokerage firms that specialize in the upscale market are offering international concierge services through affiliation with Luxury Domain, a 24-hour members-only website and telephone service. It provides travel and restaurant specialists who maintain a database of the latest happenings at the world's top hotels, resorts, spas, and restaurants. In addition to travel assistance, the concierge fulfills special requests for theatre and sporting event tickets; dinner reservations; and custom air, cruise, or rail travel.

Build credibility with designations

Earn designations because they help reinforce your positioning as an expert. If you work with a consumer who is a C.P.A., an M.D., or a PhD, they value their own designations, recognize what it takes to earn one, and respect other individuals who also have designations. A luxury home marketing designation has value as do other designations that also help build skills and enhance credibility. The Certified Luxury Home Marketing Specialist designation from the Institute for Luxury Home Marketing gives you added credibility with the affluent.

Working with NAR on the development of a report titled, *"Recruiting and Retaining Highly Successful Agents,"* I was involved in research that included a statistical analysis of what characteristics of top agents translated into additional income. In this study, the two items that had the strongest statistical correlation to making more money were the Certified Residential Specialist designation (CRS) and a high level of technology usage.

Differentiate yourself: Six steps to finding and promoting your uniqueness

In today's competitive market you must differentiate yourself from others who work in the upper tier. To do that, you must be able to capture consumers' attention, pique their interest, and create a willingness to work with you so they will say, "Yes, you're the agent for me." It's the classic advertising formula of **A**ttention, **I**nterest, **D**esire, and **A**ction. Done well, it works. The challenge is implementing the AIDA formula effectively —especially in an industry where the consumer does not always perceive that there is a difference in real estate agents and the services they deliver.

To maximize your success, you must differentiate yourself. Simply stated, you need to convince the consumer that you are unique and better able to meet his or her needs than your competitors are. If you've focused on developing the special competencies we've discussed above, you've take a big step in the right direction. Now it's time to zero in on how to build the awareness of rich buyers and sellers that you are unique and better. Here are six steps to help you set yourself apart from the crowd with a unique value proposition:

1. Understand the customer's needs. What do affluent buyers and sellers expect from you? How do you add value to the process of buying and selling? How do your services measure up? Ask your clients about their expectations of you (and how you measured up); then listen and learn.

2. Be an Expert. Keep your upper-end market knowledge current, master the complexities of the buying/selling process, and polish your communication skills. It's one thing to convince the consumer that you are unique and better able to meet their his or her needs. You must also deliver on that promise. Competence is the foundation upon which you must build your business.

3. Discover your unique abilities. You may be a powerful negotiator. Perhaps you know the market inventory better than anyone else. You may be masterful in listing properties and implementing luxury home marketing plans but prefer not to work with buyers. Maybe you specialize in luxury resort properties, golf communities, equestrian properties, downtown condos and co-ops, or know more about jumbo mortgage financing than anybody else in your office. New homes may be your specialty. Relocation buyers or high-end corporate listings may be your focus. Ask yourself what you like to do and what you do best. Sell your strengths. The things that make you unique also make you marketable.

4. Define your ideal target customer. It is difficult to be all things to all people. Look at your unique abilities and then ask yourself what customer groups need those abilities most. Analyze the opportunities in your market and then match your skills with the market segments that need what you can offer.

Remember, if you don't choose your market, your market will choose you. For instance, you might do a good job for a first time homebuyer, who refers you to a friend who also sends you business. Before you know it, first-timers are taking most of your time and representing most of your business. That's fine, if that's what you love doing. But if you'd really rather be listing upper-priced homes and have the skills to do so, you've missed the opportunity to develop your ideal market.

5. Put your uniqueness into words. Write down your unique abilities and then list how these abilities translate into *benefits* for the market segments you are targeting. Take the homebuyers' and sellers' points of view and answer their question "What does that mean to me?" For instance, you might write, "My strong negotiation skills and track record of selling luxury homes for an average of 99% of the asking price mean sellers can depend on me to help them get the best possible price for their homes." Writing down what makes you special helps you clearly define it.

6. Condense your uniqueness into a "positioning" statement (*Try to sell the sizzle, not the steak!*). Translate your uniqueness into a single statement that "positions" you in the way you wish to be perceived. Then use that statement or unique value proposition in your marketing. This will help you capture the attention and interest of prospects and give them a clear reason why they might desire to work with you.

Think about some of the positioning statements used by other products and services and you'll get the idea. Club Med's "The Antidote for Civilization" or BMW's "The Ultimate Driving Machine" are short but powerful messages. Don't be afraid to use humor. For example, "100 Pipers Scotch ... Makes Bagpipes Sound Like Music" is almost certain to stop you and make you smile. Ernst & Young conveys the extensiveness of their consulting services with the line, "From thought to finish." Dell Computer clearly puts strategy and benefits into this line, "Total accountability. On-site, online, on the phone. Easy as Dell." Yellow Freight Service keeps their delivery promise short but strong, "Yes we can."

Paul Stuart Menswear reminds us that our clothing makes a statement with two words, "Say Something." The Senior PGA Golf Tour gives us a reason to tune in to watch their matches, "These Guys Are Good." And, Hummer has sparked sales with "Hummer—Like Nothing Else."

It's a bit harder to find positioning statements in real estate. But here are a few to jump-start your thinking. A team of California Realtors who use a Q&A radio talk show to position themselves as the experts in their market use the line, "Bakersfield's Most Listened to Realtors." Do you immediately know the specialties of "Waterfront Lifestyle Specialist," or "Call the We Get It SOLD Sisters"?

In Longboat Key, Fla., agent Cheryl Loeffler uses the line "Select Cheryl with a Sea" to reinforce her name as well as her waterfront expertise. To expand on the positioning line and underscore the benefits of working with her, Cheryl's marketing materials go on to say, "She's called Cheryl with a Sea. But it's more than just a play on words. It describes why Cheryl is uniquely equipped to handle your real estate needs. Her own experiences as a Longboat Key resident and Realtor allow her to emphasize features that buyers desire: scenic views, beach access, and leisure opportunities, to name a few. She uses insights gained from her business and personal life to design the ideal marketing strategies for your property."

Define how you are unique, develop your positioning statement, and use it in your advertising, on your business card, and in your marketing presentations. Include it in your voice mail message, in your e-mail signature, and on your stationery. When you understand your uniqueness and convey it to targeted prospect groups in a benefit-oriented way, you will capture the affluent prospects' attention and also create interest and the desire to work with you. Remember the AIDA formula? All that's left is Action —ask for their business and chances are good, they'll say, "Yes!"

Chapter 10

Finding Rich Buyers and Rich Sellers

Farming

Create a farming program (yes, farming works in the luxury price ranges). Just be sure the farming pieces are consistent with the price range. Think quality, quality, quality. In addition to traditional farming techniques like just sold and just listed cards, tweak traditional farming techniques to match the luxury market. Here is a brief list of ideas to spark your thinking about farming in the luxury home market.

- Instead of recipe cards and mass market farming newsletters, send frequent market updates with statistical information about the local upper-tier real estate market. Make sure your mailing has a quality look.

- Set up a special luxury market section on your Web page. Post your statistical market updates and other information relevant to the luxury buyer and seller. Feature your upper-priced listings in this section of your Web page.

- Send your luxury market updates to the community association newsletter editors of luxury home communities.

- Volunteer to sit on other agents' higher priced open houses in return for the chance to meet prospects—this will help you break into the entry level luxury home market or help you recover if your business slides into a slump.

- Use your leftover luxury home property information sheets and brochures. Mail them out with stickers that say, "Another Sally Salespro listing SOLD!"

- Take your own or your office successes and turn them into story postcards that present a real estate challenge and explain how your expertise or firm's approach created the solution.

- Network, network, network. Trust and estate attorneys, private bankers, stock brokers, divorce lawyers, golf pros, luxury car dealers, CPAs, and country club membership directors are examples of those who are in a position to refer business to you. Remember networking with other agents who work the upper priced market is also important.

- Look for ways to interact with the affluent. If you want to get involved in your community you can contribute while creating relationships that may result in referrals. Volunteer at local museums, get involved with the arts, and participate in charity events. Farm the resulting contacts that you make.

- If you've chosen a luxury neighborhood to farm, offer to sponsor the community's Website—coordinate with the community association to post important announcements, the PDF version of their newsletter, membership information, or other relevant material that will attract residents to the community's site.

Use targeted mailing lists

If you are not sure about how to find and rent mailing lists, take a trip to your library and go to the business reference section. Ask the librarian for the *Standard Rate and Data Service Direct Marketing Book*. This book contains information on tens of thousands of business and consumer mailing lists. This book is most commonly used by advertising agencies and other marketing professionals. It may take you a while to decipher the abbreviations and marketing terminology, but it will be well worth the effort. The book will help you identify specific consumer lists, list sources, and prices. It will also identify which lists are available with e-mail addresses and phone numbers.

You can also contact an advertising agency for list recommendations (look for an agency with specific direct mail expertise), but you will pay them a fee over and above the list rental fee. Individual list brokers (sometimes called list houses) can be found in the yellow pages in major markets. They will offer you consumer mailing lists. The advantage of the SRDS book is that it compiles virtually all the list sources in one reference volume, making it easier to find the best list for your purpose.

If you decide to rent a list, be sure you understand the terms of the rental. Lists are offered for a specific number of uses or for a set period of time. For instance, you may be able to use it only once or perhaps as often as you want for thirty days. Be sure you understand the conditions or terms for the lists that you rent.

Understand that lists are "salted." That means they are sprinkled with names of people who are not single millionaires who live in Florida and own boats; instead, they are people who work for the list house. Use the list in violation of the terms, and your phone will ring with a call from the list broker or you'll simply receive another bill for use of the list.

You can create your own local mailing lists. Take the zip codes in your market and determine which ones are the highest income areas and have profiles matching the upper-tier buyer you are targeting. Sources for this information are available at the library in the business reference section. Look for the current copy of *Zip code Demographics* and the *ACORN Consumer Classification User's Guide*. Once you've spotted the zip code areas you wish to target, you can go to address/name directories to compile names and addresses of residents, or you can rent relevant lists.

In addition to these geographic lists, keep past client and customer lists, and develop lists of local executives, business owners, or other affluent individuals. Computerize your databases and keep them current for easy use. As you develop your lists, be sure to add e-mail addresses and phone numbers whenever possible. Also add the zip plus four information since it will be required at some point by the U.S. postal system.

Direct mail and e-mail work if you do it properly

An often-quoted rule in advertising is Mayer's 40-40-20 rule of direct mail, which says that 40 percent of the success of your mailing is the quality of the list; 40 percent is your offer/product/service and credibility; and 20 percent is attributable to the creative aspects of the mail piece (the copy, graphics, format, use of color, etc.). The preceding section dealt with targeted mailing lists and how to find them, so let's turn to your offer/product/service and credibility. The offer/product/service will obviously vary depending upon whether your mailing is a property offering or a general prospecting piece. If you are mailing to past clients and customers or to a group that you have consistently (and effectively) farmed, you probably already have credibility. If you are mailing to a new group, you will need to focus on quickly establishing that credibility. The professional look and overall content of your mailing will help to do that as will the use of testimonials or success stories.

Increasingly, successful agents are turning to e-mail rather than traditional mailings. The speed, savings, and higher level of attention which e-mail generates make it a very desirable marketing tool. **Most of the basics for effective direct mail can also be applied to e-mail communications**.

When it comes to the creative aspects of your direct mail, think quality. Use high quality paper, professional looking photographs, well written copy, and proof everything carefully to correct errors. An old trick of proofreaders is to read your copy through looking for errors, get someone else to read it, and then read the copy backwards word-by-word starting with the last word. It won't make sense, but you will catch spelling errors and double words as you focus on each word individually.

Here are a few suggestions to enhance the creative aspects of your mailing:

Always include a letter with a property brochure. Letters add importance and allow you to personalize the mailing. Think of a letter as a sales presentation. It should include a specific offer and invite the reader to take a specific action. For instance, "Call or e-mail me if you or someone you know would like to view this unique executive home" followed by your contact information. is a sales close or call to action. You'll want the body of the letter to be written to target the prospect as specifically as possible.

It's important to use a P.S. Advertising research tells us that the recipient of a letter first looks at the salutation, then looks to see who signed the letter, reads the P.S. and then decides whether or not to read the body of the letter. This is critical information to know when you are writing a sales letter. If the P.S. is more likely to be read than the letter itself, it makes sense always to include a P.S. and to use it to restate the key point in your letter, add another important point, or create curiosity that pulls the reader into the body of the letter.

Make your mailings YOU-oriented. As much as we might hate to admit it, we are all I-oriented. As a result, so are most letters—even sales letters. Yet the most effective marketing letters are YOU-oriented. So, here's the challenge. Write your next sales or promotional letter. Then, go back though it and count the number of I/me/mine compared to you/your. Then rewrite the letter to minimize the *I* and maximize the *YOU*. This is harder than it sounds, but the result will be a much stronger, more effective letter.

Research says longer letters are better than shorter letters. If you've ever received the sweepstakes marketing letters from Publisher's Clearing House or the subscription offerings from Readers Digest, you know that their letters go on for pages and pages. Their letters are long because long, well-written sales letters work. If you review these professionally written, copy-tested letters you'll notice the use of headlines and subheads, underscored key points, multiple post scripts and other techniques to call attention to important information. This allows you, the reader, to skim through the letter and read the parts that are most relevant to you. Incidentally, this principle of longer copy being more effective also applies to brochure copy. A straight listing of the facts may be easy to write but it is an information piece, not a sales piece.

Here's a sample cover letter for a brochure. Note the use of the P.S.

Date

Mr. Frank Jones
Success, Inc.
123 Entrepreneur Road
Kansas City, KS

Dear Mr. Jones:

Many business owners and professionals with whom I work put in long hours, work hard, and don't have much free time. As a result, they value their time at home and view their homes as private retreats. If you appreciate a home with lots of space, luxury, and comfort, you'll probably enjoy reviewing the enclosed brochure.

This wonderful home not only offers you a retreat from the pressures of work, it will make a statement about the success you've achieved. From the luxurious master bedroom suite to the unique home-entertainment theater and the convenient home gym, this home is exceptional. In the event that your business does demand your attention at home, you'll appreciate the 500-square-foot home office.

This property won't be on the market long. A successful individual will recognize its value and act quickly to enjoy its benefits. Could that person be *you*?

To take a closer look, please contact me for an appointment to tour this new listing.

My phone numbers and e-mail address are on the brochure and on the enclosed business card.

Looking forward to hearing from you,
Sally Salespro

P.S. To see other exclusive property listings in our market and across the country, visit our Web site at www.xyz.com. I can also arrange for information or showings for any of the Internet properties in which you have an interest.

Headlines make non-personalized letters effective. If you do not have names to match some of your mailing addresses, resist the temptation to use a generic salutation. Dear Homeowner or Dear Neighbor is almost as much a turn-off as Dear Occupant. Instead, think of your letter as an advertisement directed to one person and replace the inside address with a headline and the salutation with a sub-headline. Using this approach, the inside address and salutation in the Dear Mr. Jones letter above might be replaced with the following:

Date

**Going home
can mean taking
a mini-vacation.**

It doesn't get any better than this.

Many business owners and professionals with whom
I work put in long hours, work hard, and don't have...

Can you mail too much? More mail = better results. Chances are your mailings have multiple objectives. On one hand, you want to create visibility, position yourself as an expert in the upper –tier, and attract prospects. Another key objective is to sell your listings. How often do you have to mail to accomplish these goals? The answer is as often as possible. One approach is to schedule mailing much like sophisticated radio advertisers schedule ads—in waves. Ads are run frequently during a short period of time, then stop for a short while, then run frequently again. The concept is that the "waves" of frequency create awareness, and the listener doesn't realize that the advertiser has not been on the air between the waves. In other words, you could mail for four weeks in a row, not mail for three, mail for four weeks, not mail for three, and so on. Continue that pattern and you will have created an impression that you mail almost every week without having to do so. If your mail pieces are well done, they will not be viewed as intrusive.

Junk mail is a matter of the wrong timing. Much of what you mail will be glanced at and thrown away because the timing of your offer wasn't right for the reader; however, if your name has registered one more time in the reader's mind, the mail was worthwhile. Your next mailing may catch the reader when he or she has a specific need. If so, you've built visibility and credibility with earlier mailings and increased the likelihood that the prospect will contact you. The timing of the offer is important.

Recently I was standing in my kitchen opening the day's mail. What I wasn't interested in was dropped into the trash compactor. I had just glanced at a catalogue, decided that it wasn't something I needed at that time, and started to throw it away. Before the catalogue landed in the compactor, my husband, who was walking past, scooped it up and said, "Oh, don't throw that away. I want to look at it." It was the Victoria's Secret lingerie catalogue. Because I wasn't in the market for lingerie that day, it was junk mail to me. The timing was wrong. For my husband, the timing is never wrong for that catalogue. It is never junk mail.

Telephone + Mail = Higher Response Rate. When direct mail is paired with a telephone call the effectiveness increases. To make the most of your direct mail farming, at least once a year, call the people on your mailing list on the day you mail to them and let them know to expect something in the mail from you. Since you are probably mailing to a large number of people, you might break your list into 12 groups and each month call the people in one of the groups. Leaving a voice mail message will serve the purpose nicely. For example, if you send out a regular market update with statistics, you might call ahead and say, *"I've just compiled new data on what's happening in the luxury real estate market in our area. It's in the mail to you and should arrive in the next few days. If you have questions, please give me a call or send me an e-mail. If you —or someone you know—has real estate needs, I'd love the opportunity to help. In the meantime, I hope you find the market information interesting."*

If you are sending a just listed card you could call ahead and simply say, *"Today, I mailed a card to you announcing a new listing in our neighborhood. This is a wonderful opportunity to choose your new neighbors. If you have relatives or acquaintances who would like to live in the neighborhood, please pass the card along to them. And, of course, if I can help you with your real estate needs, please call."*

Ideas for mailing include:

1. **An invitation to the Internet.** People open greeting cards and invitations. So why not mail an invitation to visit your Website? Print it on nice invitation card stock and use an easy to read script typeface to address the envelope.

Sam Salespro
of
XYZ Real Estate Company
requests the pleasure of your company
on the Internet.
You're invited
to visit my Website
www.xyz.com
at your convenience
to review
fine home and estate property listings.

R.S.V.P. for information
on any of our properties
on the Internet

Sam Salesperson
Phone: 000-000-0000
E-mail: sam@ayz.com

---

2. **Market Update Reports.** Once you've gathered relevant statistical information about your local upper-tier market and the demographics of the local zip code areas you serve, keep it current and create a luxury home report. You can include the charts we've already talked about as well as some of the demographic information. Do this report on a regular basis and send it to your luxury farm areas, centers of influence, post it on your Web page, and use it with your buyers and sellers.

3. **A success story postcard.** Highlight your expertise and service with a brief story outlining how you helped a prospect accomplish specific luxury home goals.

An impossible dream?

"We were looking for a wooded, water view property and we'd almost given up. Then, we met Sally. She had a property in mind, called the owner, and sure enough, she

was able to bring the property onto the market. We wrote an offer immediately after seeing the house and had a signed contract within 12 hours. Now we can watch the ocean from our deck in the trees. Thank you, Sally!"

— Hillary and Bill Johnson

If you are interested in buying or selling, tell me your goals and I'll do my best to help you achieve them.

Call 000-000-0000 or e-mail me Sally@xyz.com.

—Sally Salespro

4. **A testimonial postcard. Testimonials are almost as powerful as referrals.** Collect them from satisfied buyers and sellers and use them in all your promotional materials. A postcard featuring testimonials is a strong credibility builder.

Sally Salespro's clients say, "It pays to work with a pro!"

"We were concerned about moving into a new city and finding a home where we could have horses. Sally gave us an overview tour, identified the equestrian communities, and then showed us the available homes. We chose the one we liked and Sally helped us negotiate the right price and coordinated a long-distance closing. With a buyers' agent like Sally, the real estate part of the move was easy.

—Eric and Cathy Welch

"When we were ready to build a new custom home, Sally helped us find the right builder and a fabulous 10-acre lot. She was masterful when it came to marketing our current home and helping us plan so that the settlement dates for both properties were perfectly coordinated for an easy move. When you work with Sally, you work with a pro."

—Olga and Vincent Hermann

Call the luxury home expert with YOUR real estate needs. Sally Salespro 000-0000, E-mail Sally@xyz.com

Consistent, targeted direct mail works. Put it to work to help build your visibility and credibility.

Video, CD-ROM, or DVD marketing

What you send through the mail doesn't have to be limited to traditional printed mail pieces. Sales and marketing professionals of all kinds are using videos and CD-ROMS to market their products and services. DVD players are also becoming more common and as DVD reproduction becomes more affordable, DVDs will also become popular promotional media.

The ability to target prospects has changed the faceless mass market of the past into audiences of one. The low cost of video and CD-ROM reproduction allows you put a powerful sales message into the hands of those prospects. When your prospect receives a video or CD-ROM, they perceive that it has high value. It is viewed less as a marketing tool and more as a gift. From the consumer's point of view, you have sent an expensive item that is commonly perceived as having entertainment value.

Research by the Wharton School of Business at the University of Pennsylvania and reported in a special supplement to *AdWeek* magazine shows:

- 90 % of those who receive a promotional video will watch it
- 85 % will watch it on the day the video is received
- 94 % are watched by more than one person
- 50 % are watched more than once
- 89 % are passed along to family or friends

A video or CD-ROM message offers other advantages. The combination of sight, sound, and motion is as powerful as television advertising but allows more time to deliver your message. A quality video or CD-ROM entertains, informs, establishes a mood, creates a positive impression, and allows you to present your sales and benefits message in a dynamic, compelling way. The CD-ROM and DVD can also link prospects directly to your Website.

A video or CD-ROM can be a powerful tool to use to generate or close prospects. If your firm has a company video or a luxury home marketing system video or CD-ROM, use it. Consider creating one with information about you, your firm, the local luxury home market, and testimonials from your upper-tier buyers and sellers

The uses of video, CD-ROM, and DVDs are limited only by your imagination and your budget. For instance, if you list homes for a custom builder, you might produce a video or CD-ROM that includes a brief interview with the builder, floor plans and renderings of the homes being built, photographs and tours of completed homes, testimonial quotes from satisfied buyers, and a link to the builder's Web page and other relevant sites. To help fund the production and distribution, the builder might produce fewer brochures (use the video piece instead) and place fewer printed mass-market ads.

Sometimes local TV stations will do affordable video production work. If you have a college or university in your area, contact the school to see which departments offer advertising, television production, or other courses attracting talented students. Talk to the professors about structuring a special project. For instance, start discussions by proposing that students work on your video for class credit and you cover direct expenses.

If you plan to mail videos or CD-ROMs, check with the post office about the least expensive way to send them. If you live in Canada, Canada Post has a special service called "Dimensional Addressed Admail" that allows the mailing of videos and CD-ROMs at special low postage rates.

E-mail Marketing

If you aren't already using e-mail as an important part of your marketing, now's the time to start. Begin collecting e-mail addresses for your past clients and customers and for your farm areas and centers of influence. Why not do a special mailing to collect e-mail addresses and to confirm prospects' interest in receiving e-mail from you? This opt-in approach allows your e-mails to be distinguished from unwanted junk e-mail or spam. The card below should get you started. The amazing technology the message mentions might be a virtual tour. You could change that phrase to say, "so I can share current information about home prices in your neighborhood."

You might also add this note to your open house sign-in sheets and other communications with prospects.

TIMES ARE CHANGING
Please share your e-mail address with me
so I can share some amazing new technology with you.
My approaches to marketing real estate and
communicating are changing.

Just e-mail your address to me at
Salespro@XYZRealty.com
or call and leave your e-mail on my voice mail

Sally Salespro
000-000-0000

As you have probably already discovered, e-mail offers tremendous advantages. It is delivered immediately and costs less than traditional mail. E-mail marketing offers you the ability to add color, sound, and movement to your communications through streaming audio and video. The direct mail ideas already discussed in this chapter can be adapted from snail mail to e-mail.

You can also create e-mail that, with a simple click, will send prospects to your Web page via a hyperlink. Have your Web page designer help you set up "landing pages" on your site. These are the pages where the user will land when clicking the hyperlink. The content of this landing page should relate to the message you have sent. For instance a message about the monthly activity in the upper-tier market should click to the full report on your Website, bypassing your homepage. A new listing message should click to your online brochure for the new listing. You may also want to ask your Web page designer to set up tracking reports for you. This is usually done by inserting a few lines of HTML code on the pages of your Website so that the number of respondents can be measured. Over time, this will allow you to evaluate the types of e-mail messages that are most effective for driving people to your web page.

HTML-formatted e-mail newsletters are offered by vendors in many markets. These newsletters are personalized for individual agents, have content specific to a market area, and look like sophisticated Web pages. Because these newsletters contain color graphics, photographs, and special type treatments, they have more impact than all-text e-mail messages. In many cases, e-mail newsletters will be sent out automatically for you if you upload your contact address list to the vendor. These newsletters will not be targeted specifically to the upper tier, so be sure the content is appropriate. Newsletters that you purchase do not replace your own market updates for the upper tier, they are a supplementary marketing tool.

Selling a country club lifestyle? Club membership directors can help you
(No, you don't have to be a member)

> Note: These same concepts can be modified for tennis or other racquet clubs, dining clubs, yachting clubs, equestrian centers, and other facilities.

Luxury homebuyers are often excellent prospects for country club memberships as well. To enhance your selling ability and your service to your prospects, target clubs in the area where you work and get to know the club membership directors.

When you have a prospect looking at homes in the club area (especially out-of-towners), utilize the membership director as a resource. This is especially effective for prospects who are looking for a country club lifestyle as part of their luxury home purchase. You don't have to be a country club member to network with the clubs in your area. Membership directors appreciate the opportunity to show their facilities to qualified member prospects, and your clients will appreciate your helping them find a club that matches their needs.

Membership directors can be sale enhancers by helping you sell the area lifestyle. They can help reinforce buying decisions and be excellent sources of buyer and seller leads. Club membership directors can be valuable networking partners. What's more, networking is easy. Contact the membership director when you have prospects interested in a country club community.

Ask the membership director to:

1.   Schedule lunch at the club for your prospects so they can get to know the club and its facilities.

When you are showing buyer prospects but need to juggle other tasks, line up some additional properties to show, or just make some phone calls. Being able to drop off your prospects for lunch at the club not only allows them to familiarize themselves with the club and meet the membership director —who will help you sell the area or reinforce a buying decision that's about to be made —it also frees you for an hour or two to take care of business. Generally the club will provide a complimentary lunch and club tour for your prospects and will usually do it on short notice.

2.   Team prospects up with members for golf, tennis, or other activities

If your prospects are looking for a country club lifestyle, membership directors will often agree to schedule tennis or a round of golf for your prospects to help them evaluate a club. They'll team your customers up with existing members who can be counted on to extol the benefits of the community and the club. This allows prospects to identify the clubs that are the best matches for them. At the same time, it demonstrates the added value service you offer.

3. Cooperate with you on a welcome or closing gift. Often they'll bear the cost and enclose your card as well as that of the membership director.

Clubs will often provide gifts for you to present to your upper-tier buyers (these are also tools for selling club memberships). Sample gifts might include a complimentary dinner at the club following property purchase, moving day picnic baskets, or congratulations cakes prepared by the club's kitchen.

4. Refer business to you.

Ask the club's membership director for buyer and seller referrals. Some people shop for country clubs before they shop for homes. The membership director is also often aware of members who are planning to leave the area. Not only can you help these homeowners sell, you can also refer them to their new locations. Provide your business cards to the membership director and ask him or her to suggest you and hand out your cards when coming across buyer or seller prospects. If you are able to get a club membership list, add it to your center of influence and farm the list.

5. Provide information about the club that you can add to your relocation packets, use to enhance your Website, and use to help position you as the country club community expert.

Add information about the clubs in your area to the community relocation packets you send to out-of-towners. Include club information in special information books you create for your upper-tier listings and add club information to your Website.

If you are in an area with multiple clubs, research the clubs and create a comparison chart to help match customers with the facilities in which they are most interested. After all, different facilities relate to different lifestyles. Develop a checklist of questions, do research, then create a club comparison checklist or matrix.

Questions you might ask about the club:

- What one-time and annual or monthly fees are charged?
- What dining facilities does the club have?
- What sports are available? (Golf, tennis, swimming, handball, squash, etc.)
- What pro and shop services are available?
- Does the club have a junior program for children?
- What member tournaments are scheduled for the various sports?
- When is the club not available for member sports (special tournaments, etc)?
- What other services are available (spa services, child care, etc.)?
- What is the dress code?
- How many members are there?
- What other clubs offer reciprocal privileges?
- If the club is in a club community, does a homeowner have priority over a non-resident for membership? Priority for tee times?
- If a homeowner sells, can he or she transfer membership to the new homebuyer?

To enhance your position as an expert in luxury home properties, consider becoming an expert in the country club lifestyle options available in your community and start by networking with club membership directors.

Add executives and professionals to your center of influence

Watch for business success stories. Everyone appreciates being recognized for his or her successes. Watch your local newspaper's business section, local and regional business magazines, and national business publications for business success stories. If you read about a local firm that wins a quality service award, a company that makes a major acquisition, a firm that goes public, a company that wins a big contract, or an executive who earns a major promotion, clip out the article. Mount it on a piece of letterhead or other paper. You may need both sides of the sheet or maybe even two sheets. Leave room to paste your business card on as well. Take this to your local office supply or teachers supply store and have it laminated. Mail the laminated article with a note and a second business card. Your note might say something like...

> *"Congratulations on your latest business success.*
> *If you're interested in moving up residentially as well, I'd be delighted to show you some of the wonderful properties available in today's market. Please contact me if you or someone you know needs real estate assistance.*
> *My card is enclosed. Again, congratulations."*

The fact that the clipping you send is laminated increases the probability that the recipient will keep it. Since your card is laminated with the clipping, your name remains with the prospect, too. Enclose a second card inside the note you write. Add this executive to your "center of influence," the list of individuals to whom you send just listed/just sold or other luxury home farming mailings.

When you or someone in your office lists a luxury home, send the property brochure with another note and card with all your contact information. You might reference the original success again. For instance...

"Your phone is probably still ringing with congratulatory calls about your new government contract. When you are ready to take a break from all that's involved in implementing your contract, I thought you'd enjoy reviewing this brochure about a simply charming English Tudor estate property that we have just listed. If you or someone you know would like to see it, I'd be delighted to arrange it. Just e-mail or call me."

After this executive has received several mailings from you, you may wish to initiate a phone contact to introduce yourself and ask if he or she would like to continue to receive property brochures from you and if there are specific real estate needs you might assist with. Remember to ask for referrals.

In most cases the business phone number is what is most easily located. You will probably reach an assistant or secretary when you call. If the staff person is hesitant to put you through and asks the purpose of your call, your phone script might sound like this:

"This is Sally Salespro with ABC Realty. I've been sending Mr. Smith brochures on some of my firm's more outstanding executive homes. I'm calling to ask if he would like to continue to receive them and if he'd prefer to receive them at home rather than at the office. May I speak with him, please?"

Or:

"This is Sam Salespro with ABC Realty. I've been sending Mr. Smith printed brochures of some of our outstanding executive homes. Many of my other executive clients have asked me to e-mail them the brochures rather than mailing them. I just wanted to check with Mr. Smith and see if he'd prefer the PDF version also.

Decide in advance of calling whether you will use a first name or the more formal Mr. or Ms. The age of the person you are calling, the standard practice in your market, and what makes you most comfortable will all be part of your decision.

Be a resource for companies that are hiring from outside the area. If you are in a large market, get to know the headhunters who work at the executive level. Offer your ability to sell the community as a resource in recruiting. Often a prospective executive will want to know more about the community and perhaps even take an overview tour before accepting a job. If you are willing to make a call to answer questions about the area, send a relocation packet of materials, and perhaps conduct an overview tour, you may be rewarded with qualified buyer prospects.

Watch for companies advertising for executive level employees on their websites or in regional or national media. Many firms advertise for executive job candidates in the national or regional editions of the *Wall Street Journal*. If you have a firm name, call and simply ask for the name of the vice president of human resources or top executive overseeing staffing, confirm the spelling of the name and the correct address. Then send a letter offering to help them recruit executive level staff by helping the company sell the area. This "you sell the job, I'll sell the area" approach can also result in business for you.

Be sure to position yourself as specializing only in executive relocations, otherwise you may find yourself looking for rentals for summer interns. If you have a relocation department or business development division in your firm, a corporate caller may already be offering these services to local companies. If so, talk with relocation about how you can earn the right to some of these referrals or take your leads to them and let them help you build the corporate relationships. Clarify up front what referral policies will apply. Even if you have to pay fees on some of the business, your center of influence with executive prospects will expand and your non-referral fee business will grow significantly over time.

Network with others who interact with the wealthy

Earlier in this book I suggested being a referral resource for services and products that the affluent need and networking with those sources. This advice can be expanded from country club membership directors (as discussed above) to include others who interact with the affluent. Teachers at private schools are often among the first to know that a family is relocating because the children announce it to their friends at school. Sales people for high end boats, marina and private airport managers, wine merchants, exclusive jewelers, interior decorators, private caterers, golf pros, riding instructors, and tennis pros all belong on your networking list. CPAs, executive headhunters, private bankers, stockbrokers, financial advisors, insurance salesmen, business brokers, are sources of executive contacts. The importance of networking can't be overemphasized.

Look for win-win opportunities in your networking. For instance, if you work in a waterfront area, network with high-ticket boat salesmen. Occasionally you might offer to enclose a brochure for an expensive boat with a property brochure mailing. Add a creative cover letter and perhaps you'll spark prospects' interest in boat and house. At the very least, you are highlighting the waterfront lifestyle you are selling and creating an opportunity for the boat seller to promote your listings. You might even ask the salesman to moor the boat in the home's boat slip during the photography session for the property brochure.

The cover letter for your house-and-boat mailing might start out with something like,

> *"If you've dreamed of living in a beautiful four bedroom home on the bay with the opportunity to step out your back door and take a romantic midnight sail, this home is for you."*

In the letter's post script or in the brochure you might say,

"If you aren't already enjoying a boating lifestyle, look no further. The gorgeous 60 foot sailboat pictured in the boat slip is available from John Jones at ABC Yacht Sales. Prefer a powerboat? John has those, too. Your dream house, plus a dream boat —life doesn't get much better. You deserve it. Call us."

Think of other ways to work together. Schedule a joint broker open house and boat tour event with the boat salesman. Both house and boat will benefit from the exposure. Schedule a VIP open event in conjunction with a big boat show and invite your center of influence, your seller's list of friends and acquaintances, and the yacht company's client and prospect list. As you begin to network, many interesting cross-promotional opportunities will appear.

One of the more interesting networking strategies I've encountered is an agent who lives in a city with a number of gated neighborhoods with gate guards. She networks with the gate guards! When you think about it, it makes sense. She says that people will pull up to the gate and ask if there are properties for sale. The gate guard will tell them that unfortunately, he can't let them in but will then give them the agent's card and indicate that she specializes in gated communities and would be happy to show them what's available in this community as well as other gated communities. The agent keeps the gate guards happy with cookies and other goodies left over from open houses and occasional pizza delivery. She told me she closes millions of dollars worth of business each year as a result of gate guard referrals.

Work the custom builder market

Call on luxury homebuilders. Often smaller firms build just a few homes each year and don't have sales staff on site. If you can't convince them to list with you, ask them to refer you to their buyers who have homes to sell. You may even want to offer to hold a weekend open house for a builder's new home, or advertise a builder's home to capture calls from prospects. Be sure to include builders on your list when you mail your market updates. Joining your local chapter of the National Association of Home Builders is a good way to build your visibility in the new homes market.

A very successful agent in Los Angeles built her business by volunteering to hold open houses for builders' custom homes. Today she does over a hundred million dollars worth of business each year and her client list reads like a Hollywood who's who.

Chapter 11

Working with Rich Buyers

Pre-qualifying buyer prospects:
Are these folks for real?

In some situations, sellers may require that a prospect's ability to purchase be confirmed *before* a showing appointment is even scheduled. (Celebrities and others concerned about security may insist upon pre-qualification to help weed out curious sightseers.) This can sometimes be solved by having prospects pre-approved for their mortgage. If time precludes this or if prospects plan to be cash buyers, a letter from a private banker, brokerage firm or other financial entity confirming assets or credit available is another common way of handling the issue of pre-qualifying prospects

Pre-qualifying your buyer prospect is important regardless of price range. Don't jump to conclusions about an individual's ability to buy based on the car they drive or how they dress. Don't be hesitant to ask where the assets to purchase a home will come from or to request letters or other asset confirmation from a banker, broker, and/or other financial source. Some agents ask all prospects to meet with a loan originator for pre-qualification before they show property. This is an excellent strategy.

Develop a script to ask for financial information. For instance,

"As you can understand, many sellers of luxury properties require that only pre-qualified prospects be given access to their

*homes. To ensure that I can show you the homes that you'll want—
and need —to see before making a smart buying decision, I must
verify in writing your ability to buy in the million-dollar range.
We can handle this easily by setting up a brief pre-approval
appointment with a lender. Or, if you prefer —or plan an all cash
purchase —you can have your banker, broker, or other financial
institution simply provide a letter verifying that you have the
necessary assets. Which approach would you prefer?"*

Be sure you have a system for requesting and collecting
written asset verification information. You may want to develop
a standard form or letter which your prospect signs granting a
financial entity permission to give you information regarding
assets.

While this approach is standard in the upper tier, industry
speaker and author Michael Merin suggests that having them
pre-approved for a loan may be an even better strategy.

In his training sessions, Merin, recommends having affluent
buyer prospects pre-approved. Invariably, he says a nicely mani-
cured hand is raised and the agent explains that in her market,
agents would never think of asking their wealthy buyers about
their finances. It just isn't done

It should be done, Merin emphasizes. "If an agent is asking
some buyers whether a lender has pre-qualified them in the last
60 days and is not asking others, the agent is violating fair housing laws by treating potential clients differently.

"Asking the question may also set the stage for more effective negotiation for your home buying client. Your buyer may
chuckle and reply that money will not be a problem and refer
you to an accountant, broker, or private banker for a verification of assets. However, simply including this letter with your
offer can alert the seller that your prospect is wealthy."

Merin believes that in some situations this announcement of
wealth may affect your negotiating strength. "Just as a pre-approval erects a wall between the seller and a weak buyer's financial troubles, allowing you to negotiate more effectively for
your buyer, a pre-approval allows a wealthy buyer to negotiate

without having to reveal his or her full financial strength. Urge your wealthy buyer to become pre-approved," says Merin, rather than providing a letter confirming substantial assets. "In my experience, rich buyers often have a friend or close acquaintance who owns their own bank and can easily have a legitimate pre-approval letter prepared. Few sellers will come far off their asking prices for your buyer clients when the sellers learn that the buyers are rich. This is not just a cash buyer, the seller will conclude, but a wealthy client."

In some states, agency laws and regulations allow you to write the offer and keep the buyer's identity anonymous. This can work if it is a common practice, but beware of falling into the same trap. To the extent that it is common for only wealthy buyers to submit offers anonymously, you may raise that same flag announcing the wealth of the potential buyer.

Merin believes that almost as important as convincing the buyer to become pre-approved is advising the buyer to work with the right lender —someone who will satisfy the listing agent's questions without revealing too much. "When called by the listing agent," Merin suggests, "the lender should answer that the ratios or credit scores are acceptable and the buyer's cash reserves are sufficient rather than revealing what the front-end and back-end ratios are, what the credit score is, or how much money the buyers have available. A pre-approval commitment (not just a pre-qualification letter) with the right lender is a powerful negotiating tool."

Unless you are a tax accountant, leave the discussion of the tax implications of a purchase to the experts. As you work in the upper tier, you will develop relationships with experts in real estate related fields. If your affluent clients need specialized assistance, you can refer them to knowledgeable practitioners who hopefully will reciprocate by referring their clients with real estate needs to you.

Showing buyer prospects

The basic principles for showing a home are the same regardless of price, but recognize that busy, affluent buyers may have no patience for agents who haven't previewed homes before showing them. Be certain the homes meet the condition requirements of the buyer and that they are consistent with what the buyer is looking for —just being in the right price range isn't enough. If you feel that a buyer needs to see a home that may not meet their exact criteria but has other features that you think make it a viable option for the prospect, be sure you explain up front. Otherwise they'll think you aren't listening.

It is important to note that in some markets, very expensive properties may have sellers who ask that the listing agent be present at every showing. In this case, the listing agent may even assume the responsibility for showing the home and all of its special amenities.

If you are pursuing a listing in a market where "listing agent must be present to show" is common, recognize that this will require extra time and commitment on your part. If you plan to have your assistant help with this, be sure you know your state's requirements regarding appropriate tasks and licensing for assistants.

Florida agent Wayne Adams (who works the Tampa Bay luxury home market with his wife Joyce, who is also his business partner) prefers to handle the showings of their listings and understands how to sell in the process. Recently he and Joyce listed a million-dollar waterfront home. Another agent called to schedule a showing, telling Wayne that the prospects had looked at 50 homes over a year's time and were satisfied with none of them. After many questions from Wayne about what the buyers liked and disliked, the showing was confirmed for later in the day.

When the agent arrived with buyers in tow, Wayne took them into the foyer and said, "I understand that you have looked at 50 homes during the past year. This is the last one you need to see because..." The next two minutes were spent with Wayne outlining how this home had everything they liked with none of the features they disliked.

When Wayne finished, the husband said, "Wayne, you are aggressive."

Wayne's laughing answer was, "I haven't been called that low key in years."

After orienting them to the home, Wayne guided the prospects through the property pointing out the details that supported his conversation in the foyer. Within 10 feet of the door, the wife said, "This is nice." A little later the husband commented, "This is good value for the money." (Buying signs!) The next morning, the buyers' agent faxed a cash offer for almost full price with just an inspection contingency. The property closed in two weeks.

Wayne is right when he says that bringing qualified buyers to the door is just the first step in a successful marketing program for a listing. A second major step is a having a showing and selling plan once they are in the home. This assumes that you have done some information gathering about what the prospect's priorities are and what likes and dislikes they've expressed when viewing other properties. Controlling the showings of your listings takes time but it actually gives you the opportunity to SELL the home to prospects by demonstrating how it meets their needs.

Expensive homes still need to be presented effectively and staged to sell.

Chapter 12

Working with Rich Sellers

Questions to ask when setting the listing appointment

The initial information-gathering step for a listing is important. When you're on the telephone setting up the appointment for the listing presentation, think about some key questions in addition to the basic ones. For instance, the answers to the questions listed below are valuable to know before you call on the homeowner and begin the listing process.

When was this house last on the market?

This will quickly identify expired listings and also help you pinpoint the last time the property changed hands so you can more easily research the last sales price.

Do you know which builder built your home?

Do you know which architect designed your home?

Did you do your own interior design or did you use an outside designer?

The answers to these three questions may have an impact on the value.

Has the house had media coverage in the past?

Perhaps the home was a show home for a charity, was featured in a national home design magazine, or has important historical significance. You can do some quick research and go into the listing presentation with information that that will help you establish quick rapport and make you more knowledgeable about the property. The question regarding media coverage may also reveal disclosure issues. If something happened in the house that caused the media to report on it, then you can sensitively probe a bit and find out what happened.

Is there anything else I should know about your home?

I call this the Magic Question. It will often reveal the sellers' hot buttons. They will tell you about the home's features that they think are most important. These may be the same features the next buyer will find appealing. Sellers may describe special features or improvements they believe will add value to a property—perhaps a new kitchen, which they anticipate will return more than they paid for it 12 months earlier. Forewarned is forearmed. You may also get some surprising answers.

An agent in Ohio told me a story about asking the magic question, "Is there anything else I should know about your home?" as she was setting up the appointment for a listing presentation. The seller on the other end of the phone line said, "The house is haunted. We have a ghost; but don't worry, it's a friendly ghost." He went on to tell her a very charming and romantic ghost story that dated back to Civil War times.

The agent said, "That's a wonderful story. When I list your house, would you be comfortable if I called the lifestyle editor of the local paper? With the ghost story you just told me, I think we could get some great publicity for the house. How would you feel about that?"

The seller thought it was a great idea and gave the agent the listing. The agent called the editor of the paper's lifestyle section who agreed that the story would make an interesting feature article. On a Sunday morning, the paper featured an article with photographs about the haunted house. The sellers were quoted, as was the real estate agent who was referred to as an expert in the marketing of historic and upper priced properties —great visibility for the house and for the agent. Also mentioned was the fact that the home would be open for the afternoon.

The line to get in the open house went down the sidewalk, down the street, and around the corner. The agent and her helpers had to count people as they let them in because they didn't want more than a certain number in that house at any one time. Not all those attending were qualified prospects. However, on Monday morning in offices, in elevators, and probably in kitchens with neighbors visiting, the conversations went like this, "Did you happen to see the article about the haunted house? Guess what, we went to see it." That kind of word-of-mouth sells properties. In fact, the house sold within a week of the article having appeared.

So ask the magic question, "Is there anything else you'd like me to know?" You'll discover the sellers' hot buttons, reveal a disclosure issue, or you may find a marketing hook you can use.

Send information in advance

You have the appointment to discuss listing the property. Now's the time to further position yourself as a true professional. Put together a packet of information about you, your firm, and (if you have one) your special luxury home marketing program. Recruit a responsible neighborhood teenager to deliver it before your appointment. Have your delivery person carry a clipboard, hand the prospect the packet and have them sign for it. This reinforces the importance of the material.

Some of the national upper-tier marketing programs have video or CD presentations that introduce prospects to their programs. These information/sales presentations are excellent tools to use in this way. A firm in the Boston area boxes their luxury home program video with chocolates, gourmet coffee, and a couple of coffee mugs bearing the company logo. The box is gift wrapped and delivered to the prospect with a note from the agent. A pre-meeting package could also include your personal brochure, information about your firm, testimonial letters from happy sellers, and a current market update.

One visit or two?

When working with unique custom homes, your listing presentation will require two visits, one to see the property and a second visit to present your market analysis and pricing recommendation. On your first visit, tour thoroughly. I know that you can blitz through a house in no time at all and get the information that you need. You do it every time you go on the tour of your office's new listings, right? Fifteen, twenty, thirty agents traipse through a new listing and if the owners are there, they are standing at the open door amazed that that many people can go through the house so quickly and come away with any information at all. But you can; that's your business.

Don't do that in the first visit of your listing approach. Let your seller lead you through the house, tell you the stories, point out the gourmet kitchen, talk about the antique paneling in the library, or describe other features while you take notes and establish rapport and credibility. As you tour, you'll want to acknowledge the positive features and make note of the negatives.

Try to get the seller's pricing expectations on your first visit. An agent who works in Atlanta calls this first visit of a two-visit listing approach the "you don't sit down visit," because, she says, if you sit down the seller will not let you up until you tell them what you think the house is worth. She organizes her tour of the property so that she always concludes the tour at the front door. Just before she steps across the threshold to leave, she turns around and she says, "Oh by the way, what are your pricing expectations for this property?" The seller usually turns the question around and responds with. "You're the expert; what do you think?"

At that point it may be tempting to give a ballpark figure. Resist. Don't even give a range, because what's going to happen? The seller will take the high point of the range, carve it in stone, and never let you forget it. Instead, you want to sidestep the issue of price until you are ready to discuss it. You probably already use a script along these lines, *"I would never do you the disservice of taking price lightly. It's just too important. I want to go back to the office, thoroughly review the comparable listings and sales, give this some serious thought, and when I come back tomorrow, we'll talk about my recommended list price. We'll also talk about the marketing plan for your property."*

If, at this point, they still have not given you their pricing expectations, one approach is to say, *"While I am searching for comparable listings and sales, what comparable price range do you think I should start in?"* Their answer will help reveal their pricing expectations.

CMAs and executive summaries

Finding comparable properties for unique, luxury residences can be difficult. Don't attempt to price an upper-tier custom property on the first visit unless you are very, very knowledgeable. Instead, note the property's condition, special characteristics, and amenities. Then, research comparable listings and sales and prepare a complete market analysis.

You CMA should be thorough. When possible, include photographs of the sold and current comparable properties and be prepared to discuss the features and amenities of each property.

Remember that many of the homeowners in the luxury price range are business owners, corporate executives, and other professionals. These individuals are quantitative, bottom-line-oriented, and busy. Why not prepare a thorough market analysis and then create a one-page executive summary that has a couple of sentences on each comparable, summarizes the market conditions in the relevant price ranges, and presents the recommended list price? The businessmen and women with whom you work are used to receiving their information in this form and will relate to it immediately. They can cut to the chase and then delve into the details.

Price versus selling time

Ask the seller's pricing expectations on your initial visit or when scheduling the appointment. They will probably turn the question around and say, "You're the expert, you tell me." Develop a script to help you gather the information you need without having to discuss list price until you're ready.

Also take the time to explain the relationship between selling time and price to the seller. You might show them a price and selling time continuum and ask them to place themselves on the price and time line based on their priorities

Highest price_____▼_____Shortest Selling Time

Based on their priorities, where would they put themselves on the timeline?

The answer will give you insight into which is most important to them and help them understand that the highest price and shortest selling time are usually trade-offs.

Differentiating yourself at the listing presentation

Remember that first impressions are very important. You must look professional and project confidence and professionalism. Don't wing it; be prepared. Then, to differentiate yourself and your listing presentation, you must sell three things:

1. Sell yourself and your competencies. Why are you the best agent for the job? How will your experience, training, market knowledge, pricing ability, contacts, enthusiasm, etc., help you accomplish their objectives? (This is about *why* you can accomplish *their* real estate goals more than it is about you — be confident, but leave your ego at home)

2. Sell your company. Your firm is a most likely a well-known company in your market; leverage this visibility and credibility. Talk about the company, its resources, advertising, relocation connections, size, and how these things work to help you assist them in marketing their home. If your firm is part of a national brand, referral network, or has a luxury home network affiliation, this may be perceived as an advantage. Explain the benefits to the prospect.

3. Sell your marketing plan for the property. Luxury home sellers want to know exactly how you plan to market their homes. Saying "I'll promote your home" isn't enough. They want to know how, where, and when. The most effective presentation of your plan is in writing.

Obviously, your recommended list price is an important aspect of your listing presentation. As has already been mentioned, pricing can be very difficult when dealing with custom homes because there are so few comparables. The more knowledgeable you are about the market, the better able you are to peg the selling price.

When you work in the highest price ranges, homes are unique. This makes it very difficult to do a one-step listing presentation unless you are already very familiar with the property. Expect to do a two-step presentation. The first visit will be to tour the property, the second visit will be to discuss your suggested list price and the proposed marketing plan.

Polish your presentation

Start with confidence. You only have about 30 seconds to make a first impression. Walk into your meeting with energy and a smile. Although you need to be very careful with cultural differences if you are working with an international clientele, in general, some good rules for successful interactions include: Look prospects in the eye. Shake hands firmly. Make sure you have the correct pronunciations of all names. Thank them for the opportunity to present your service and be prepared.

Be prospect oriented. While it is important to establish your credibility, the focus of your presentation should be the prospects' needs, not all your past accomplishments. Ask questions about their goals and expectations and take time to listen. Also personalize the presentation for each seller and home.

Respond to their needs. Be sure that you address the questions and concerns they express. Although a listing appointment is a presentation, it should also be a dialogue. You gather information from them and then explain how working with you will help them meet their needs.

Be organized but flexible. Know what you are going to say, stay focused, and don't waste the prospects' time. If the prospect appears ready to make a decision to list with you, close. You don't have to give your entire presentation every time. Keep going and you may talk yourself out of a listing.

Use technology. Demonstrate that you have the technology savvy to get the home sold by using tech tools in your presentation.

Follow-up ideas
for after the listing presentation

Ideally, the completed listing presentation should culminate in the immediate listing of the property. You've worked to establish rapport with the sellers. You've toured the home, letting the sellers point out the property's special features. You've discussed *how* you can help meet their selling objectives and *why* you're the agent who can best assist them. You've dealt with the issue of price. The final step in the presentation is *asking* for the business. However, if you are one of several agents presenting, and the decision is not an immediate one, you'll need to follow up.

Before you leave the listing presentation, acknowledge the importance of their decision and reinforce why you are the right agent for the job. You'll want to develop your own scripts, but here's an idea to start with:

"Selling your property is a big decision, and I understand that you want to choose your agent carefully. All I ask is that when you sit down to make your choice that you remember four things –

- *my enthusiasm about your property,*
- *my commitment to do a good job for you,*
- *the customized marketing plan that's ready for implementation,*
- *and that I can put the power of an effective luxury home marketing program to work for you."*

Then follow up:

- Have a "thank you for the opportunity" note or letter delivered to the homeowner as soon as possible after your presentation.
- Reiterate the four reasons to choose you in your note.

Keep following up:

- Create a sense of urgency with a deadline:*"If I can begin marketing your home this week, we can just make the advertising deadline for the next issue of such-and-such publication. I've attached some suggested ad copy for your review and suggestions. Let's finalize the listing paperwork and begin the marketing process."*
- Share a success story: *"Another ABC Realtors luxury home property SOLD! 1234 Main St. sold for 98% of the list price. Let me put the power of my luxury marketing program to work getting your home sold."*
- Recognize that some of the same techniques you use to follow-up with sellers in other price ranges can be adapted to the upper tier. Take what already works for you and tweak it.

Chapter 13

Marketing Luxury Listings

Positioning the property

The first step in marketing a property is to define clearly what it is you are selling. You need to develop a positioning statement for the house—a brief summary statement of the key features and benefits offered by the home. Ask yourself why someone would buy this home. This positioning statement will be your springboard for developing your marketing strategy and for developing your marketing materials. Here are three examples of positioning statements:

- **Contemporary Florida Home in Gated Golf Course Community**

  Room for big family, perfect for entertaining

  Well located for Tampa, St. Petersburg, Clearwater, and Airports
  Panoramic Waterfront views
  Your own private beach and boat dock
  Huge rooms, high ceilings, all the amenities
  20 minutes to city center

- **English Tudor design, new construction**

  Elegant five-bedroom on five wooded acres
  Equestrian community
  Top-rated school system

- **Manhattan concierge condominium with park views**

  Health club, rooftop pool, and theatre room
  Two bedrooms, 24th Floor
  Upper West side

Setting the marketing budget

While one percent is often a number quoted when agents talk about a marketing budget for a luxury property, there is no magic formula. A key budgeting decision factor is the current market situation. If the market is hot, the property is very desirable, and the expected selling time is short, you may not need to advertise in publications with extended deadlines or order brochures with long production times. A fast-moving market generally requires a lower budget. Conversely, if extended and extensive marketing is anticipated, a more substantial budget will be necessary. Rather than using a formula to set the budget, the market conditions and the salability of the house should determine what you invest in marketing.

Remember that it is important to track the days on market by price range so that you have a clear idea about how long it is currently taking homes to sell. Before you commit to your marketing plan, be sure you have a listing term long enough to give you an adequate amount of marketing time. If homes in the $2 million dollar price range are taking an average of 220 days to sell, a six-month listing is not a reasonable listing period. You'll want to ask for at least 12 months.

Steps for developing your marketing plan

After looking at a property and reviewing market conditions, you probably have an approximate marketing budget in mind. Set that number aside for a moment.

1. Take a blank sheet of paper and ask yourself, "If I could do anything I wanted to market this property, what would it be?" Allow yourself to be as creative as possible and list all the things that come to mind.

2. Next, review your list and prioritize it by asking yourself, "If I could only do one thing on my list to sell this property, what would it be? If I could do two things? Three?... " Continue prioritizing until you have ranked all the items

on your list. Make a new copy of your list with the marketing ideas listed in sequence as prioritized.

3. Now take each item on your list and calculate what it would cost to implement that idea. Keep a running total. At some point your total will equal the marketing budget you have in mind. Draw a line separating those ideas from the others. Everything above that line is your standard marketing plan. If you have marketing ideas left on your list, remove any ideas that cost too much based on the marketing value they offer. Then divide the remaining list in half based on cost.

You now have marketing ideas in a list, broken into three sub-lists or chunks. The first is your standard marketing plan. The second chunk is your plus one percent plan, the third chunk is your plus two percent plan. (Assuming of course, that these tasks can be accomplished for the additional one and two percent.) This approach gives you the flexibility to offer three commission choices based on the level of marketing. For example, you might have a six, seven, or eight percent commission plan for your seller to choose from.

Even more important, this technique is likely to generate a more creative and effective marketing plan than if you just listed the first few marketing ideas you can come up with and then realized that you had already reached the reasonable budget maximum.

This three-tiered plan can be used a variety of ways. You and the seller can agree to implement the second and third aspects of the plan if the property has not sold within a set period of time. This approach to planning also sets the stage for effectively handling the question: "This is an expensive property; you are going to cut your commission, aren't you?" Your answer might be, "Actually I am going to give you your choice of commissions. The marketing plan we have just looked at is a six percent marketing plan. I can also show you a seven percent and an eight percent plan which include additional marketing efforts."

This technique for developing a marketing plan also gives you a basic marketing plan (which you can afford to implement at the commission you have negotiated) plus a list of additional marketing ideas that you might implement at the seller's expense. When the seller reviews your marketing plan and asks, "Aren't there other things you can do to market my home?" You are prepared to say, "Yes, I have a list of a number of other marketing efforts we can implement and I will make a commitment to you. I will add the other tasks to the existing marketing plan, I will implement them for you and it will only cost you $X." In some markets, agents negotiate receiving these additional marketing dollars upfront from the seller. These dollars may or may not be refundable to the seller at closing depending upon what is negotiated.

Procedures!
A system for implementing
your marketing plans

As soon as you list a luxury property, begin implementing your marketing plan.

1. Take all the elements of your plan and break each into specific tasks. If you are doing a full-color property brochure, you might have these production tasks: decide on size, format, and quantity; develop theme; write copy; schedule photography; have client review the copy and photographs; coordinate layout with brochure company; approve final proof; confirm delivery date.

2. Take your task list, assign deadline dates, and identify who's responsible (this may always be you).

3. Next, create a property-marketing calendar and enter all the tasks on their deadline dates.

4. Each day, as you make your to-do list, enter the tasks that will keep your marketing plan on track. Recogniz-

ing that this is a crazy business, you will often have days when you don't accomplish anything on your to-do list. Instead you are scrambling to hold a transaction together, working with a last-minute prospect, or preparing for a listing presentation. When that happens, you need to take the next available opportunity to catch up on your marketing plan tasks.

5. When you have a few minutes ask yourself what you need to do to get your marketing plan implementation back on schedule. Then do those tasks. If you don't deliver on your marketing as promised, you'll quickly find yourself out of business in the upper-tier market.

Keys to creating a successful property brochure

Your property brochure is a written sales presentation. Its effectiveness relies on good copy and photographs that showcase the home and the lifestyle it offers. Your positioning statement for the property will help you determine the brochure's theme, key points, and headlines. The brochure is also an opportunity to reinforce your positioning in the market, so include a thumbnail photograph of yourself with your contact information.

Expensive properties demand high-quality brochures. There are national vendors who specialize in full color real estate brochures and can refer a professional photographer to assist you. Local printers who specialize in short-run color work may also be an option. Compare prices and turn-around time before selecting a vendor.

It may not be necessary to do a full color brochure. A well-designed black and white or duotone brochure on quality paper may be just as effective if your copy and photographs are top notch. If you are not a good writer, find a freelance advertising writer or college advertising/marketing major and pay a small fee to have your copy edited. It will cost lots more if you ask them to create the copy from scratch. Write it yourself, list all the amenities and features, and then let the expert add some sales pizzazz. Some brochure companies will perform this service for you.

If you order color brochures, negotiate with the printer for color postcards, too. Once the brochure is on the press being printed, it is a simple matter to print postcards as well. It requires a bit more press time and paper, but since the highest cost is preparing, inking, and then cleaning the press, it saves money to print everything you need at once. Design your postcards when your brochure is designed.

Remember to prepare or stage your listing for the photo shoot just as you do for an open house and be on hand to direct the photographer. Plan the time of day for the photo session based on the specific property. Schedule the exterior photo shoot to coincide with the time of day that the front of the house is illuminated and not in the shadows. If you have a home with lots of shadows on the facade because of landscaping, you might ask the photographer to schedule the shoot for a cloudy day when shadows won't show (if timing allows) or when the light is soft (twilight). If you do a sunset or twilight shoot, turn on all the house lights for a warm and welcoming golden glow.

Using the Internet as a marketing tool

Put your information on your firm's Website

You should have an agent profile on your firm's Web page. Think of this profile as a brochure promoting your services. Write benefit-oriented copy that is less about you and more about how you can help buyers and sellers achieve their real estate goals. Use this opportunity to highlight your expertise in the upper tier with testimonials and success stories.

It may be more beneficial to be on the company site than to have an independent Website. The value of a site comes from the traffic it generates and the results it delivers for you. Unless you are able to drive traffic to your individual site through lots of advertising, you may get more visibility on the company's site, especially if your market has implemented listing reciprocity and your company site features all the MLS listing inventory. The ability to display all the listings will help attract eyeballs.

You may choose to be on your company site and have your own Web page as well. If you have your own site:

- Get your site listed with search engines like Yahoo, Google, AskJeeves, Dogpile, and others.
- Link to other real estate Websites
- Do keyword searches to find other related sites and link to them
- Research e-zines (online magazines) that relate to the affluent or luxury homes and advertise. Try *http://www.ezinesearch.com* or *http://ezineseek.com* to find e-zines.

Put your listings online

Since the affluent are users of the Internet, you'll want to be sure to put your listings online. Think of the Internet as an opportunity to create an electronic property brochure. Include a complete, well-written description of the property. Don't use real estate abbreviations; spell everything out. Feature multiple photographs of the property. Virtual tours may add value if they are well done and showcase the property effectively. Floor plans add value and should be included for new homes and for urban condominiums and cooperatives. Be sure to keep pricing and property status information current. Make it easy for prospects to contact you for additional information or for a showing appointment. Respond promptly.

In most markets, multiple listing systems offer listing reciprocity to broker members. This allows all the MLS listing inventory to be featured on participating brokers' Websites. If your firm participates in reciprocity, you will want to be sure that each property description you submit to MLS is as effective with prospects as with agents. This also makes photographs of the property more important than ever.

Look for other opportunities to feature your listings online. Many real estate publishers will post your listing on their Websites when you advertise in their publications. Be sure to ask for exposure on the Web as well as in the printed publication.

E-mail new listing announcements to prospect groups

Keep your affluent center of influence updated on your new listings with short e-mail messages. Create an online brochure for each of your listings. Include photographs and complete descriptions. Link the e-mail message to your online brochure.

Establish Websites for the communities you farm

Creating a Website for a neighborhood is both a community service and a powerful promotional tool for you. The site can include community photos, statistical information on real estate, a community events calendar, homeowner association information, school calendar, and, of course, information about your services and listings. Be sure to keep the Website current.

To create your site, start by setting up the URL (or Web address). Go to *www.register.com* and do a search for the neighborhood name you wish to use. You can register the name online for a reasonable fee. Ask your Web-page developer to design a simple, inexpensive site for you. Coordinate with the local homeowners association by offering to post their newsletter, community event announcements, and other information on the site. Promote the neighborhood Website in your farming materials, in relevant advertising, and property brochures.

Your neighborhood site is a great place to post your regular market updates with information on the neighborhood housing market. This helps reinforce your reputation as the neighborhood expert.

Network online

The Web is brimming with special interest websites. Some of these Websites offer the opportunity to network directly with potential prospects or to advertise your listings inexpensively. For instance, if you specialize in equestrian properties, do an Online search for sites that relate to horse ownership. Check out the sites for opportunities to post a notice or add a classified ad about your listings. You may find mailing lists, chat rooms, links for your Website, and numerous other networking possibilities. The Internet is a fabulous resource, use it!

Use your personal digital assistant to access MLS

Technology can help you provide better service. Special software for your personal digital assistant allows you to download your MLS data into your Palm Pilot or other PDA. This allows you to access listing information on the go. If you are out with a buyer who has a question about a home you happen to drive by, you can check MLS to see price and current status. You can pull up the contact information and call for an appointment if the buyer wishes. You will also have the ability to pull up comparables.

Having the MLS data at your fingertips can save time and help you deliver the level of service your affluent clients and customers expect.

Open houses or VIP events

At the entry level of the upper tier or with new home properties, it may be desirable to hold traditional open houses. In the higher price ranges, security issues and the brevity of the qualified prospect list will make invitation-only VIP events more appropriate. If a special event to showcase the home is part of your marketing plan, you will want to talk to your sellers about adding friends, acquaintances, and business associates to the list of invitees. In addition, you will want to consider if there are special target groups based on the location or amenities the home offers.

Use your creativity in planning the event. Is there a special theme that might increase attendance? Is there an opportunity to do a joint event with a charity? Co-hosting with a carefully selected non-profit group generates free publicity and can increase attendance and exposure for the home. The non-profit group also brings important resources, including people who can serve as room monitors while the house is open. Be sure sellers know to put away small valuables and breakables during the event. A local museum, historic preservation society, opera, or symphony group would be an example of a non-profit organization that might plan a members-only event with you.

Be sure to schedule an open house for brokers and personally invite the agents in your community who specialize in the luxury home market. This broker open house can be a good way to gather feedback about the property. Create a small card that you can give to real estate agents as they arrive to see the home. Jokingly tell them it is their ticket to leave the house. Keep questions short and simple so that it can be filled in quickly. Have some extra pencils handy. You may get more honest feedback if you make responses anonymous by providing a bowl to hold completed cards.

1234 Luxury Lane

Your expertise and opinion are valuable to me.

Please take a minute to give me your honest feedback with regard to this new listing:

Pricing	__Excellent	__Good__Fair__Poor
How well it shows	__Excellent	__Good__Fair__Poor
Chances you will show	__Excellent	__Good__Fair__Poor

Comments_____

_____

Other marketing ideas

Keep your eyes and ears open for other ways to promote your listings. For instance, if you have a unique property designed by a well-known architect, has celebrity owners, or is priced in the multi-million-dollar price range, you might consider contacting *Architectural Digest*. The magazine has a monthly residential real estate section featuring very special homes for sale. This is a content as opposed to advertising section and is a beautiful vehicle for promoting truly exceptional properties with international appeal. *Architectural Digest's* homes for sale section is called "Estates for Sale: Editors Select Properties Around the World" and features exotic properties as diverse as a villa in a Venetian lagoon, a home on the French Riviera designed by the architect of the Eiffel tower, and the penthouse of a Manhattan Beaux Arts Bank building constructed in 1907 and converted to residences in 2000. If you have a world-class property, this special magazine section is an option to explore.

Chapter 14

Delivering Quality Service

Quality in a product or service is not what the supplier puts in. It is what the customer gets out and is willing to pay for...customers pay only for what is of use to them and gives them value. Nothing else constitutes quality.

—Peter Drucker

Remember that the buying and selling *process* really doesn't differ much by price range; however, the luxury market is more demanding of your professionalism, communication skills, and ability to get the job done. You are dealing with successful individuals who have high expectations for themselves and who will hold you to the highest service standards. Remember that today's affluent consumers have service expectations created by other industries that set service benchmarks. Your service will be measured against those benchmarks. In short, when you work with rich buyers and rich sellers, you'd better be good!

In Chapter 9, we looked at the importance of positioning yourself as unique and better able to meet the needs of rich buyers and sellers. Creating this perception in the minds of your clients and customers and then delivering on that promise will mean that buyers and sellers will want to work with you, will be willing to pay a full or premium price, and will be eager to refer you. Quality service is an important part of living up to the promise of being unique and better.

Before we talk about the specifics of creating value for the consumer, it is important to understand the three stages of success and how they relate to value creation.

Understand the three stages of success

In real estate, success comes from understanding and meeting the needs of your clients and customers. As you develop your ability to do that, you will pass through three levels of success.

The agent in the first stage of success is average. He or she has basic skills and generally doesn't focus on specific market segments or work to build special competencies. Because the average agent doesn't define and target market opportunities, he or she must be all things to all people and handle whatever business presents itself. After a while, the average agent's market tends to define itself. For example, if you sell a first time homebuyer and do a good job, chances are that client will refer a friend. The next thing you know, you are working with lots of first-timers and working in neighborhoods of entry-level homes. This might be terrific, unless you would prefer to be working in higher price ranges and specializing in golf course properties.

Success Stage I

THE AVERAGE AGENT

↑

Acceptable Service

↑

"All Things to All People"

↑

Basic Competence

The next level of success is illustrated by the Top Producer who has targeted special market segments and has developed market and customer knowledge specific to those niches. At this level, the agent better understands how to meet customer expectations and provides really good service.

Success Stage II

THE TOP PRODUCER

Meeting Customer Needs

Really Good Service

Developing Target Markets

Special Expertise

Strong Competence

Agents at the third stage rate "best in the business" recognition. They not only have targeted special niches, but have developed so much expertise and market knowledge that they are unique. As a result of these unique abilities, they are able to offer additional value and special services that exceed client expectations. Success stage three is the level you want to attain.

Success Stage III

THE BEST IN THE BUSINESS

Surprise and *WOW* Customers

Outstanding Service

Ability to Create Value

Defined Target Markets

Unique Abilities

Focus on creating value for the consumer

1. Clarify expectations

The time to establish expectations is during your initial interaction with a buyer and during your listing presentation to a seller. An excellent way to do this is with a service guarantee checklist that outlines what you'll do step-by-step for the buyer or seller. This checklist can be even stronger if it outlines the steps and attaches a *benefit statement* to each point. Keep your guarantee realistic. Don't raise expectations you can't meet. Instead, under-promise and over-deliver.

Here's my guarantee to you:

- ✓ I'll prepare a competitive market analysis with information on current homes for sale and comparable sold properties. This information, plus advice on pricing to maximize buyer interest and bottom line returns for you, *means* you'll have the information you need to make the best decision on pricing your home.
- ✓ Together we'll tour your home and discuss how to "stage" it so that it can be shown most effectively
- ✓ Your property will be entered into the Multiple Listing System, *which means* information about your home is available to virtually all the agents in the market. This maximizes the exposure for your property.
- ✓ Etc.

As you walk them through your service guarantee, you'll also be discovering how their expectations match up with the list. In doing this, you'll discover issues before they can become problems. For instance, if you have an assistant who often handles calls and specific tasks for buyers and sellers, your clients may have questions about why they can't always deal directly with you. It's important to answer questions like those at the beginning.

You'll also want to be sure your expectations are communicated. If you expect sellers to leave the house during showings, you'll need to express that and perhaps explain why. If the best way to communicate with you is on your cell phone or via e-mail, now's the time to let them know that. Sharing expectations also opens the communication process.

2. Instill confidence

Recognize that good communication and personal integrity will help ensure that the consumer feels good about working with you. Here are five things that will go a long way toward helping you establish credibility and create confidence in the consumer's mind.

- Show up on time
- Listen
- Do what you promise
- Admit mistakes and fix them quickly
- Remember that manners matter

3. Care about your client and work to connect

Be personable. We all want to work with someone we like. To some extent we are all selling a relationship; because, in an initial interaction, it is easier to evaluate a relationship than it is to measure competency. Ask yourself if you would want to work with you.

4. Create a positive experience

How can you enhance the experience for the customer? What can you do to lessen the stress, make the process more interesting, or add an element of positive surprise? Also look for vendors who are focused on ways to add value. For instance, Houston-based Stewart Title Company has a special division for closing fine homes and estates and offers an environment and service level to please the most demanding client.

5. Say thank you

Manners matter. When you are trusted by a client to help with his or her home sale or purchase, a verbal thank you is required. A hand-written note and thank-you gift are always appropriate as well. An annual thank-you event for your customers serves the dual purpose of showing your appreciation for their business and helping you maintain contact.

6. Ask how you did

You may think you did a good job, but what does your client think? You won't know for certain unless you ask. A short written survey allows him or her to give you feedback in a way that promotes honest comments. Be sure to also ask for the nicest thing he or she can honestly say about your service and permission to use his or her quotes in your marketing. Then add the positive comments to your testimonial book or other marketing pieces.

7. Stay in touch, stay in touch, stay in touch

Make it a point to contact your past clients and customers on a regular basis. Let them know you are available to help with their real estate needs and ask for referrals. The goal is to build an ongoing relationship.

Chapter 15

Meeting Special Challenges

Targeting the upper tier in a small community

Smaller markets may not have many luxury properties. In this case, your goal is to capture as many of them as possible — to become the dominant agent in the upper price range.

Tie the luxury home target market to other market niches that might logically mesh with it. For instance, if high-priced properties are clustered in a particular neighborhood that also has homes in other price ranges, work the neighborhood. Maybe your luxury buyers and sellers are primarily corporate executives. If so, target the corporate and relocation markets. Find a geographic farm area priced just below the upper tier and hope to capture buyers moving out and moving up. If your top properties are waterfront or golf course homes, focus on those special markets even though not all the properties will be upper-tier. In summary, combine related niches with the upper-tier niche and you'll have a solid strategy.

Marketing historic real estate

Many markets have historic properties that may command high prices. *The National Trust for Historic Preservation* offers real estate professionals a variety of resources. A special program, open to real estate agents regardless of company affiliation, includes training covering architectural styles from early colonial through art deco. It provides education on historic preservation legislation and ordinances, tax incentives, and the requirements for inclusion in the National Register of Historic Places. If you work in a market with numerous historic properties, this training will strengthen your expertise in the historic home niche. Course participants are also given a six-month membership in the National Trust, a certificate of completion, and approved verbiage to use in personal promotion. Agents who attend the program are listed with their contract information on the National Trust's Website, *www.nationaltrust.org*. For information and course dates, call 973-496-5628.

The National Register was authorized under the National Historic Preservation Act of 1966 and is administered by the Department of the Interior's National Park Service. It is the nation's official list of historically significant structures. A National Register designation mandates that a property must be considered in the planning of federal or federally assisted projects impacting the registered property, and qualifies that site for financial assistance from the government when preservation funds are available. Properties may qualify for special mortgages, grants, and tax credits.

To learn more about the National Register, visit its Website, *www.cr.nps.gov/nr*. It includes information on the more than 70,000 listed properties and information on how to nominate a property.

Working with other experts as part of your client's team

When dealing with affluent individuals, you will often be just one of the experts they employ to assist them in their real estate decision-making. They may want to turn to their CPA and estate planner to discuss the tax consequences of a home purchase, or for advice about how to hold ownership based on estate and inheritance issues. An attorney, tax accountant, business manager, private banker, estate trustee, or financial consultant may also be part of the decision process. Working though the maze of players and their responsibilities can make the buy/sell decision process more complex and require your patience.

If you're lucky, the client will manage this process. If he or she looks to you to do that, then you'll have to keep things moving forward diplomatically. Recognize the role that everyone plays in the process and avoid stepping on toes while you work to facilitate the process for the client. Keep communication open and flowing among participants. Help keep everyone focused on the client's goal. Be sure you understand the contribution the client expects each participant to make and be sure the client understands the time frame in which things must be finalized to keep a scheduled closing (or negotiation) on track.

Success in the luxury home market is about positioning yourself as THE expert and then delivering on that promise—which means knowing the luxury market better than the competition and getting results for buyers and sellers. Once you've done that, your reputation will create opportunities and referrals. In the meantime, work on building your competencies, look for the unique skills and tools that may give you an edge and use them.

Selling luxury homes at auction

Auctions are no longer associated with distress sales or bargain basement prices. A well-planned real estate auction can generate premium prices for homes. Sellers of unique or extremely expensive properties that are difficult to appraise and have high monthly costs may want to consider working with you and an auction company in hopes of a speedy sale and maximum price. A quick auction sale can reduce marketing time and consequently cut an owner's carrying costs such as mortgage expense, maintenance and insurance expenses, and taxes. Properties in high-supply markets may also benefit by using an auction to capture attention. Tony A. Isbell, president of Houston-based Realty Bid International, Inc., has sold approximately

10,000 commercial, investment, and luxury residential properties during the past 16 years. He says the practice of auctioning luxury residences has skyrocketed since the middle of the 1990s.

Isbell says there are there are three common types of auctions. Generally, auctions are assumed to be *reserve auctions* unless explicitly advertised otherwise. In a reserve auction, there is no minimum bid. The seller is not obligated to sell the property but has the right to accept or reject the highest bid. In an *absolute auction*, a sale is guaranteed. The property will go to the highest bidder, regardless of the price. The absolute auction usually attracts the most bidders because prospective buyers are hoping for a bargain. With lots of bidders, a competitive bidding environment is often created, which results in a top price. A *minimum bid auction* is just that—only bids above a minimum advertised amount are accepted.

Auction houses will work with a listing agent to plan and conduct a successful luxury home auction. This technique is growing in popularity. A study conducted for the National Association of Realtors predicts that within eight years, almost one third of all real estate sold will be through auctions.

Isbell describes the typical auction event as starting six to eight weeks in advance with advertising, usually paid for by the seller. Free press coverage is generally sought for the auction as well. A property brochure is created and mailed to a target prospect list developed by the real estate agent and the auction company. The property is available for scheduled showing appointments and should also be available for viewing on the Internet with virtual tours and multiple photographs.

The day of the auction, the home is open, and bids are accepted from registered bidders who typically must post a five percent deposit in certified funds. When the winning bid is established, the bidder must sign a purchase contract and set a closing date, typically within six weeks. All other deposit checks are returned to other bidders.

Not only are auctions growing in numbers, they are moving online. General consumer auction sites such as eBay have grown in popularity. In fact, The National Consumer League estimated that by the end of 2000, nearly one third of adults who had been online had participated in an online auction of some sort—approximately 35.6 million people. Realty Bid International decided to capitalize on this online auction success and now offers Internet auctions for luxury home properties on its *www.RealtyBid.com* website.

Michael Keracher, Realty Bid's executive vice president of sales and marketing, says, "In the past when I would visit owners of luxury properties, they had several concerns about traditional auctions including privacy issues, the intrusiveness and hype of an auction, plus costs and risks. Realty Bid's new Internet platform allows an auction to happen in cyberspace, not at the property. This is less intrusive and is a huge privacy benefit to sellers. It is also about half the price of a traditional auction. An online auction takes place over 30 days instead of just a few minutes. If the property does not meet its minimum price, the auction can simply be extended."

The Internet auction is an interesting new marketing tool that may be a match for selective luxury properties and sellers. For more detailed information on how luxury home auctions work and what the real estate agent's role is in the auction process, find links to more than 100 auction companies on NAR's auction information site, *www.narauctionsource.com*.

Chapter 16

Getting Started in the Luxury Home Niche

New to luxury home marketing? Share a listing with an experienced agent

You've decided to target the upper tier and you've found a good listing prospect, but you're concerned that your inexperience and lack of a track record in the higher price ranges may hinder your ability to capture the listing. Why not find an experienced upper-tier agent with your company and offer to partner on your first transaction? You provide the prospect and do the work; he or she provides credibility and serves as your mentor for this transaction.

Naturally, you split the fee. To avoid misunderstandings, be sure to agree upon the responsibilities and the fee-sharing formula upfront.

You and the experienced agent should carefully plan the listing presentation and work together on the market analysis and the marketing plan. As an agent starting in the luxury market, you will probably want to perform these planning tasks yourself under the guidance of the experienced pro. This will help you maximize your own learning.

Since the prospect is yours, you'll want to take the initial lead in the listing presentation and then hand off to the more experienced agent. You should:

➤ Thank the sellers for the opportunity to meet with them about marketing their home,

➤ Introduce the experienced agent and highlight the agent's credibility and track record of success in the upper-tier arena.

➤ Discuss *why* and *how* you will work together as a team to market the property. Stress the benefits of having both of you working for them.

➤ Use "we" terminology to reinforce the fact that you'll be working together as a marketing team.

The presentation of the market analysis or CMA and the discussion/negotiation of marketing price with the seller will probably best be done by the experienced agent

In presenting the written marketing plan, you may to wish to highlight who will be responsible for implementing each marketing task. You will probably assume most of the responsibility for implementation.

Highlight the experienced agent's ability to network with other agents who specialize in the higher price range (locally and internationally), and let your partner explain why that is so important. Emphasize his or her contacts in the community and how that center of influence will be utilized in your marketing plan.

It is not necessary that the presentation be evenly divided, but each team member should have the opportunity to establish credibility and rapport. Clearly position the two of you as a team providing added value to the client. Be sure your client knows who will be the primary contact.

Remember that first impressions are very important. You must look professional and project confidence and professionalism. Don't wing it; be prepared. Then, to differentiate your, your listing presentation must sell these things:

• **Your joint competencies.** Why are you the best agents for the job? Your teammate's experience, training, market knowledge, pricing ability and contacts can help accomplish the seller's objectives Add your enthusiasm, hard work, and creativity, and you have a super sales duo. (This is about *why* you can accomplish *their* real estate goals more than it is about you—be confident, but leave your ego at home)

- **Your company.** Talk about the company, its resources, advertising, relocation connections, or other important features, and how these things work to help you assist them in marketing their home.

- **A written marketing plan customized for the property.** Luxury home sellers want to know exactly how you plan to market their home. Saying, "I'll promote your home," isn't enough. They want to know how, where, and when.

You'll probably want to let the experienced agent ask for the listing. You can hand the client the pen!

Here's a sample script explaining the joint approach (just to get you started).

"My goal is to do the best possible job for you. To maximize my marketing power, I've asked Sally Salespro, who is one of the top luxury home experts in our community, to act as a special consultant in the marketing of your home. Sally and I will work as a team. Her extensive experience, expertise, and market contacts combined with my aggressive marketing will be a powerful combination. Together we can implement a marketing plan designed to market your luxury property effectively.

"An aggressive newer agent with the time and energy to really focus on getting the job done for you...PLUS an experienced agent with incredible market savvy and contacts in the luxury home market...PLUS a special marketing plan for your home...that's a combination that will get you the results you want."

Agent's Getting Started Work Sheet

What's Your Action Plan?

What will you do to jump-start your business in the upper tier...or to take it to the next level? Here are some ideas to spark your own planning process.

Step I. Analyze the upper tier market: Gather the key statistics

(If there are other agents in your office who are also targeting the upper tier, team up for the information-gathering step...divide the tasks and share the results.)

1. Define *your* market area
2. Identify top 10% of sales/listings in last 12 months
3. Break this top 10% into logical price bands
4. Calculate for each price band
   - Number of sales (buyers)
   - Sale to expiration ratio
   - Average days on market
   - List to sales price differential
   - Percent new versus resale
   - Average term of listing (this may be a "best guess" estimate)
5. Make charts to illustrate these statistics
6. Ask your company to begin geographic tracking

(Where do buyers come from? Keep these records by price range.)

Step II. Analyze the upper-tier market: Profile prospects

1. Profile the upper-tier buyers & sellers in your market.

Are they corporate executives, second-home buyers, young high-techies, sports celebrities?

What's the old money, new money mix? What do you think

are their buying motivations? Which neighborhoods do they choose?

2. Which categories or profile groups will you target? Why?

Rank the groups by opportunity level. Do you already have an entrée to any of these groups?

How should you position yourself?

3. How can you begin to interact with your prospect groups?

Networking opportunities?

Step III. Analyze the upper-tier competition: Who's doing what?

1. Identify players in upper price ranges—which agents are your strongest competitors?
2. What are strengths & weaknesses?
3. Affiliations and special upper-end programs?
4. How can you differentiate yourself?
5. How can you network effectively?

Step IV. Line up your tools

Identify any special tools available from your network and/or company.

Decide what other marketing resources you need.

Step V. Set some specific goals

How will you know you are making progress after 90 days? Six months? The first year?

What is your specific production goal for the first year?

Step VI. Develop a plan to market yourself and develop prospects

Remember there's no one right way to do this. Build on *your* strengths

How do you want to be positioned? What will differentiate you? Work on a positioning statement that clearly states in writing how you wish to be perceived in the luxury market. Build your self-promotion around that concept.

You plan might start with some or all of these things...

1. Volunteer to hold other agents'(or builders') listings open
2. Send "we have listed, sold, or participated in the sale of" cards to the geographic areas or centers of influence you've targeted (you don't have to be the lister, but do coordinate with the lister/seller. He or she benefits, too! Be prepared to explain how.
3. Create on-going market updates with the statistical info you've developed and mail them to your prospect groups. Provide information on market trends to the media, too.
4. Watch for business success stories and send article plus note and card.
5. Develop networking relationships with country club membership managers, gate guards, architects, decorators, builders, and others who interact with the affluent. Develop a resource list for the affluent.
6. Target move-ups. Work FSBOs and expireds in the price range just below the upper tier or in the bottom of the upper tier if your market offers that opportunity.
7. Develop a personal brochure positioning you as an expert in the upper-price market.

Priorities Worksheet for Agents

Make a commitment to yourself to get to work now!

What are the FOUR most important things you can do now to begin or to expand your upper tier business?

➤ **Priority No. 1:**

_____

Specific tasks/deadlines:

_____

_____

_____Deadline_____

Estimated cost:_____

➤ **Priority No. 2:**

_____

Specific tasks/deadlines:

_____

_____

_____Deadline_____

Estimated cost:_____

➤ **Priority No. 3:**

_____

Specific tasks/deadlines:

_____

_____Deadline_____

Estimated cost:_____

> **Priority No. 4:**

_____

Specific tasks/deadlines:

_____

_____

_____Deadline_____

Estimated cost:_____

In 60 days, I will be on track IF:

_____

_____

_____

OTHER IDEAS FOR GETTING STARTED:

_____

_____

_____

_____

NOTE: See Chapter 20 for an action plan for broker/owners and managers to use to build a luxury home program at the office or company level.

Chapter 17

The Second-Home and Resort Markets

Second-home market offers opportunities

Just as the luxury market is a small part of the national home sale market, so is the second-home market—5.5 percent. But depending upon your location, it can be a large part of your local market and represent excellent opportunities to work with affluent buyers and sellers.

Data extrapolated from The National Association of Realtors' *Profile of Home Buyers and Sellers 2002*, show there were 359,000 single-family second-home sales in 2001. This was down 4.8 percent from a record 377,000 sales in 1999. No data is available for 2000 since the study is conducted every two years. Even though the 2001 statistic registered a decline, the number of second home sales was the second-highest sales total since the study began in 1989.

Sales of Second Homes, 1995–2001		
Year	**Number**	**% change**
1995	296,000	NA
1997	345,000	16.6 %
1999	377,000	9.3 %
2001	359,000	- 4.8 %
Source: National Association of Realtors, Press Release, 2002		

Although number of sales slipped in the second home arena in 2001, the median price jumped sharply. According to the NAR survey, the median price of a second home in 2001 (both new and existing) was $162,000, which is up a whopping 26.8 percent compared to the 1999 median price of $127,800. For the first time, the median price of a second home also surpassed the median price of all homes sold.

David Lereah, NAR's chief economist, said that a big consideration in the growth of the second home market in the late 1990s is that a large pent-up demand for second homes was released in 1997 following the tax law changes that allow most sellers to exclude up to $500,000 in capital gains from taxation. "This freed buyers wishing to trade down to a smaller primary residence and also use some of their equity to purchase a second home, sometimes as a trial retirement home," Lereah said. "In hindsight, a surge of sales in 1999 was no surprise, given the fact baby boomers were entering the peak years during which people typically buy a second home at the same time that many investors were looking to diversify portfolio assets."

Baby boomers are still the most likely second-home buyers. The median age of second-home buyers in 2001 was 46, and the median income was $77,700. Seventy-two percent of buyers were married couples, 10 percent were single males, 10 percent were single females and 6 percent were single/unmarried couples. Note that single buyers represent about 26 percent of second-home buyers, up from 21 percent in 1999. Don't forget that affluent singles can be great prospects.

If boomers are the buyers, why the modest sales decline in 2001? "The mild recession in 2001 had a dampening effect on discretionary spending, resulting in a slight pullback from the second home market," Lereah says.

The shift of dot-coms to not-coms and the resulting skid in the stock market probably did cause many affluent individuals to look at their portfolios and feel less wealthy (they were). Some may have decided to put dollars into real estate; others were cautious about making any investments.

Those who invested in residential real estate have done well, according to the Mortgage Bankers Association of America's *Economic Fact Sheet, 2001*. Over the three years from 1999 to 2001, home prices increased at an average annual rate of 8.1 percent, trailing only the stock market in total return on investment. During 2001, stock returns fell 3.4 percent while house values increased 9.1 percent. Using variance in returns as a measure of risk, housing returns have the lowest risk, with the exception of mid-2002. That should make investors in homes happier than most stock market investors.

Another possible factor in the drop in number of sales is a lack of inventory. "Nationally, we've had tight housing inventories generally. Professionals specializing in recreational property say there aren't enough vacation homes to meet demand in many areas, causing prices to rise sharply," Lereah said. "The availability of vacation homes is reported to be especially tight in coastal markets."

NAR reports 5.5 percent of all homes sold in 2001 were second homes; it estimates half of those are for recreational use and half are held as rental investment property.

The U.S. Census Bureau estimates there were a total of 3.5 million seasonal (recreational) homes throughout the United States in 2000, up from 3.1 million in 1990. NAR projects there are comparable numbers of second homes held as rental investments.

NAR forecasts that the demographic impact alone from large numbers of people in their 40s and 50s entering the second home market could potentially add 100,000 to 150,000 housing starts each year through the end of the decade. However, given the limited availability of desirable locations that can be developed, builders active in this market indicate actual construction starts have been about half of that level. Lack of inventory is boosting prices and often cutting selling time.

Although we tend to focus on luxury properties when we think of second homes, the typical recreational property tends to be more modest. Nonetheless, there are many above average second residences that fit the profile of the luxurious home. It is these properties upon which upper-tier experts will wish to focus. However, in some resort markets, combining these upper-tier properties with other second home properties is a good strategy since there will be similarities in the two segments— out-of-town owners who are part-time residents, prospects from common geographic areas, issues regarding renting the properties, etc. If you can develop your competencies and services around the special needs of the second-home owner, you will also be positioning yourself effectively to capture the high-end prospects as well.

Vacation homes can be found in every state and region, with the most popular locations by the water or in the mountains. Not surprisingly, the Census Bureau reports the states with the largest number of recreational homes are those with large populations: Florida, California, Texas, and Michigan. However, the highest percentage of vacation homes can be found in Maine, Vermont, New Hampshire, Alaska, Delaware, Florida, Arizona, Wisconsin, Montana, and Hawaii. Most second-home owners prefer to be within a day's drive of their second home.

Chapter 18

Trends in the luxury market

Demographics bode well for luxury niche

Increasingly, Realtors recognize that demographics have a significant impact on total housing demand and the type of housing buyers purchase. Over the next two decades, we can expect some significant shifts in demand as a result of predicted demographic changes.

On one hand, new demand from the traditional homebuyers — married couples in their late 30s and early 40s with children —will decline as married households with children decline in numbers. On the other hand, demand sparked by single women, single men, empty-nest boomers and other non-traditional households is expected to grow.

These changes have already started. First time homebuyers are increasing as a percentage of total home purchasers as non-traditional buyers move into the marketplace. Single purchasers already represent 29 percent of all homebuyers. Unmarried couples represent another 5 percent of buyers.

Baby boomers (those born between 1946 and 1964) are primary drivers of home demand. As the youngest of the boomers move into prime home buying years and progress in their careers (earning more), we should see a growing luxury home market. Affluent older boomers moving into their mid-fifties may also fuel demand for move-up luxury homes or second homes.

The product purchased is also beginning a subtle shift. Urban/center city and rural homes are increasing as a percentage of the total homes sold, while suburban purchases are slipping as a percentage of the total. Many expect this to continue as empty-nest boomers gravitate to new lifestyles, and other categories of childless buyers find urban lofts and other downtown residences attractive. One wild card in this new appeal of many urban centers is terrorism. Since September 11, 2001, some people are reconsidering center cities and looking at other alternatives. Whether this will slow down or squelch the "back-to-town" trend remains to be seen.

The accompanying charts, with their Census Bureau projections, may offer insight into overall housing demand and luxury home demand over the next two decades.

U.S. population projections by age group (in thousands)

Year	Total	Under18	18-34	35-44	45-64	65+
1995	262,820	68,743	65,789	42,514	52,231	33,543
2000	274,634	70,783	63,491	44,659	60,992	34,709
2005	285,981	72,509	68,430	38,521	78,848	39,408
2020	322,742	77,603	72,853	39,612	79,454	53,220

Percentage change for 1995 to 2005

Total	Under 18	18-34	35-44	45-64	65 +
8.8%	4.7%	-1.9%	—	36%	7.8%

Percentage change from 1995 to 2020

Total	Under 18	18-34	35-44	45-64	65 +
22.8%	12.9%	10.7%	-6.8%	52%	58.6%

Source: *U.S. Bureau of Census, Current Population Reports*

Statistics
Lovers'
Bonus

Projected households by types, 1995 to 2010

	1995	2000	2005	2010	Change
FamilyHouseholds*	68.4	71.7	74.7	77.9	13.9%
WithChildren	32.6	33.1	32.7	32.2	-1.2%
WithoutChildren	35.8	38.6	42.0	45.7	27.7%
SingleHouseholds	24.3	26.2	28.3	30.7	26.3%
Other	5.0	5.4	5.8	6.2	24.0%
TOTAL	97.7	103.2	108.8	114.8	17.5%

* This category includes households of married couples and other households comprised of related family members.

Source: *U.S. Bureau of the Census, Current Population Reports*

Luxury Home Trends

Bigger homes, smaller lots

More square footage is the holy grail of today's buyers. Homebuyers want larger rooms and more rooms. Often this extra interior space comes at the expense of lot size. The footprint of the house is larger relative to the size of the lot. In most markets you can see this trend in action if you have exclusive neighborhoods where tear-downs occur. A home purchase will result in the old home being scraped off the lot and a new larger home being constructed. Even though the small house concept is widely discussed by architects and others, the luxury homebuyer is buying or building BIG.

Architectural design consistency

The new luxury homes being built today have more architectural design integrity. Instead of combining styles or putting a facade of a particular style on the front of a home and leaving the other sides style-less, builders are using architectural styles more consistently both outside and inside the home. There is also a trend toward using designs appropriate to the location. For instance, look for Spanish mission home designs rather than French chateaux in the desert.

Home offices

The desire for a home office transcends price range. In the average-price home, the office may be a computer desk built into a bedroom or an office nook on the landing at the top of the stairs. In a luxury home, the office may be as elaborate as a wood paneled office suite with conference area, room for a staff person and office machines, kitchen facility, multiple phone lines, and fast Internet connections. If you're marketing a home without a home office, it's worth thinking about how existing space might be adapted for an office.

Housing moving to town

The concept of living and working in a downtown environment where you can walk to shopping and restaurants is catching on. Entire new town centers with retail, office, and residential spaces are springing up in suburban areas that never had downtowns. City developers are converting office or retail to residential lofts and building new townhouses and other residences downtown. Generally there is a mix of housing types and price ranges with the luxury home well represented. The National Homebuilders Association's House of the Year in 2000 is a good example of the back to town trend—a three-story townhouse in downtown Portland (OR).

This trend back to town still appears to be healthy in most markets despite the terrorism in New York in September of 2001. In fact, special subsidy programs in New York are helping to restore demand in the areas of lower Manhattan that were affected by the World Trade Center tragedy.

Concierge Programs

Affluent individuals are accustomed to using the services of the concierge in a fine hotel. Dinner reservations, theatre tickets, limousine arrangements, and other services are available quickly and easily from the concierge. Increasingly, concierge services are being introduced to the real estate industry in two different forms. Luxury condominium and cooperative buildings offer concierge services similar to those of a hotel. Brokerage firms are also developing special customer service programs that may be labeled as concierge services but are actually one-stop-shopping programs for homeownership services.

For the affluent prospect, time is money and the ability to buy, obtain a mortgage, close, arrange homeowners' insurance, and have utilities connected all with a single point of contact is added value. If a brokerage also offers expanded homeownership services to include recommended vendors and coordination of things like pool and yard maintenance, home repair and renovation plus appliance discounts and other product and services savings, so much the better. More brokers are developing these programs or plugging into national one-stop-shopping programs such as HomeLink to address the customers' desire for an easier transaction and on-going service.

Ready-made mansions

A new trend in high dollar home sales is the instant mansion—new homes that come furnished, decorated, and ready for occupancy. For the busy professional or the buyer who isn't confident about his or her own taste, a ready-made home is an easy solution.

Big city trends: instant penthouses and "building up"

As demand for in-town housing grows in many markets, developers have had to get creative. When space in desirable buildings is fully utilized, "building-up" or the addition of an instant penthouse residence provides new income options for building owners or more space for owner/occupants.

First Penthouse Ltd., a Swedish company, specializes in ready-made penthouses that are installed on top of existing buildings. The company buys roof space, does the necessary preparation work for installation (electrical, plumbing, etc.) then builds the new penthouses in their Swedish factory. The exterior of each penthouse is designed and finished to match its host building. When completed, the penthouse is lifted into place by cranes and interior finish-out is done on site. The building owner shares in the profit. The firm has installed a number of residential units on top of London's historic Albert Court apartment building.

A similar concept involving penthouse additions is the onsite construction of a new top floor —referred to as "building up." The New York City condominium market is home to many new penthouses as a result of building owners' desires to offer new construction and spectacular city views while maximizing their buildings' revenue.

Big city trends: Designer condominiums

Looking for ways to differentiate luxury condominium developments, developers are turning to big name architects and marketing the "signature" buildings they design for a premium. Does the architect make a difference? A Michael Graves-designed building in Miami's trendy South Beach commanded a premium of about 20 percent more than comparable units in other buildings. It's like putting Polo on a shirt. The Richard Meier-designed twin towers in New York City's Greenwich Village report Calvin Klein and Martha Stewart as early buyers. Both snatched up penthouse units. Major cities, including New York and Chicago, host new buildings carrying names like Philip Johnson and Robert Stern. The Philip Johnson-designed building planned for New York's Soho district may —according to the developer Antonio Vendome—be marketed as "habitable sculpture" through an art dealer rather than a real estate broker.

Chapter 19

Advanced Marketing– Lifestyle Segmentation

We've looked at the differences between old money and new money prospects, but there are other ways to segment the rich buyer and rich seller. As you read in Chapter 9, ACORN, a consumer classification system used in sales and marketing, identifies and characterizes specific groups like Top One Percent, Successful Suburbanites, Urban Professional Couples, Prairie Farmers, and Thriving Immigrants. This information is valuable because it will help you evaluate potential farm areas and help you identify the most likely buyer types attracted to particular neighborhoods.

In real estate, you can also often spot specific affluent lifestyle groups by how their homes are decorated. Understanding lifestyles can give you some insight into motivations, attitudes, what will appeal to prospects, and how to sell them more effectively.

Here are some affluent lifestyle groups I've observed. See if you recognize any of your clients and customers on this list. You may be able to add some other lifestyle groups. The important point is that lifestyles influence the types of homes people want and can give you some insights into how to make your interactions with them more effective.

1. **Travelers**

   These folks love to travel and their excitement about the places they've been is reflected in their daily lives and in their homes. Their decorating is eclectic. A Moroccan table, an African mask, Indian candlesticks, a rug from Santa Fe, and a Russian icon might accessorize the same room. They use bright, spicy colors. Their approach to home design is not about fashion; it is about preserving the memories of their travels. They want a home that showcases their travel treasures. A custom home that has international design features may appeal to them. They may have multiple homes and be concerned about security when they travel. Letting them tell you their travel tales is a quick rapport builder. When you are out for the day showing travelers, take them to lunch at the most exotic ethnic restaurant in town.

2. **Flamboyants**

This group not only wants to be noticed, they want their wealth recognized. Their decorating will be lavish and extravagant. (Think gold bathroom fixtures.) They often gravitate to the trophy house with a long list of special amenities. Entertaining is important to them. They wear initialed brand clothing, drive luxury cars, drop names, and know what's hot and what's not. They can be great fun to have as clients. Dress up to work with this group. Pre-qualify them and show them your most flamboyant properties in the "best" neighborhoods. Plan lunch somewhere trendy.

3. **Spartans**

Keep it simple might be the mantra of the sophisticated Spartans. For this group, minimal is more. An urban loft or a sleek suburban contemporary may have great appeal. Good design and effective use of space is important. Don't show them anything too elaborate or cute. White, black, lots of glass, open floor plans, and large rooms, will appeal to this prospect type. Simplicity will carry over to how they dress. Don't take them to a tearoom for lunch—a sophisticated bistro would be better. The decor may be more important than the food.

4. Romantics

At the opposite end of the spectrum from the Spartans are the romantics—we could call them the Martha Stewart set. Their homes are decorated in soft colors, with lots of romantic, feminine touches. They are family-oriented and warm. They want their home to be a luxurious, nurturing environment. Show them the charming English Tudor, the white-columned colonial, or the sprawling beachfront family compound. Do go to the tearoom for lunch and ask to see the grandchildren's photos.

5. Outdoor Lovers

These prospects love nature and bring it indoors. Their homes will incorporate natural materials like slate, stone, logs, and exposed wood. The view will matter to this group. Panoramic water or mountain views, settings in the woods, and other outdoor environments will appeal. This group is likely to have a second home in a beautiful locale. They are concerned about protecting the environment, will want to know if the neighborhood has recycling facilities, and may appreciate the home with grounds that have reverted to a natural state. Ask where they'd like to have a second or future retirement home and refer them. Take them to an upscale vegetarian restaurant for lunch or get gourmet carry out and eat in the park.

6. Collectors

This is a small group, but easily recognized. These prospects are collectors and their home is the museum or showcase for their collection. They may collect paintings, antiques, sculpture, cars, or any number of other things, but whatever it is, they have a lot of it and it takes center stage in their homes. If possible, look at their collections to get a better sense of their needs. Match the homes to their display needs —lots of wall space for art, high ceilings and spacious rooms for large-scale antique furniture, and so on. Take the time to learn a little about what they collect, ask a few intelligent questions, and they'll open up and tell you more about their needs. Have lunch in the museum dining room.

Chapter 20

Marketing Tools and Action Plan for Brokers

This chapter contains an informational/sales piece that will help you explain to a prospect why it makes sense to select an agent (like you) who specializes in the luxury market. This chapter also contains a checklist for broker/owners or managers who wish to build a luxury-home marketing program for their firm or office.

The document below is designed to be used as a part of your listing presentation or in the initial interaction with your buyer prospects. Its objective is to help you get the business by reinforcing the criteria for selecting a luxury home expert. For a downloadable copy that you can print out, visit *www.LuxuryHomeMarketing.com.*

Seven tips for selecting the right real estate agent to help you buy or sell a luxury home

Laurie Moore-Moore
Executive Director
Institute for Luxury Home Marketing

Not all good agents operate effectively in the upper-tier market. It is a market segment that requires special competencies. Here are some general guidelines for choosing an agent to assist you in the upper-tier residential marketplace.

1. If you have an agent with whom you've successfully worked in the past, and now you are looking in a new part of the country or different corner of the world, **ask that agent to refer you to a luxury home specialist in the new locale**. Upper tier agents network, often attend national or international meetings, and many have earned special professional designations and have contacts with others with the same credentials.

2. **Look for market knowledge and real estate skills**. Not only should your agent know the city or area you are interested in, he or she should be knowledgeable about the price range you've targeted. A luxury home expert should be able to discuss the amount of inventory available, the average number of days a property is on the market before going under contract, the number of sales in the last 90 days, and the list to sales price ratio—*all by price range*. The more knowledgeable the agent is about the upper tier market, the more valuable he or she can be as a resource for you. When you schedule your first meeting with a prospective agent let the agent know you want an overview of the market conditions based on your price range. **A solid track record of success is a clear indicator of market savvy**. Don't choose an agent based on country club membership, the kind of car he or she drives, or similar criteria. Do choose your agent based on the answer to the question: "Does this agent have the competencies necessary to help me accomplish my real estate goals?"

3. **Notice special designations and ask what they mean**. Some real estate professionals have earned their broker's license, which means they have had additional training and a certain amount of experience. The Institute of Luxury Home Marketing awards an international designation (Certified Luxury Home Marketing Specialist) to agents who meet both education and performance requirements. You'll also find agents with educational designations from the National Association of

Realtors. A few real estate companies offer special luxury home designations to their agents. These credentials add credibility but they don't always mean that you should ignore a newer agent without designations. A bright, creative newcomer who's willing to work hard, do the market research, and has targeted the upper tier can provide excellent service, too.

4. **If you are selling, ask that the listing presentation include a specific marketing plan for your property**. Don't assume that the best marketing plan is always the most expensive. Listen to *why* the agent has included each element of the plan. If the home is very expensive or the buyer is likely to come from outside the area, a luxury home magazine may be an important part of the plan. Recognize that in a hot market, there may not be time to do a full color brochure. Your agent should outline the plan and explain it. Look at the quality of the marketing pieces the agent has used in the past as part of your evaluation process. Some agents will have access to special luxury home marketing systems with special marketing pieces that add to an agent's toolkit.

5. **If you are selling, don't let an agent "buy" your business**. Choosing an agent based on who suggested the highest list price is counterproductive if the house is overpriced. The agent doesn't set the price—the marketplace does. If your home goes on the market as an overpriced listing, agents and their prospects will quickly move on to other properties that offer more value relative to cost. Will they come back if the price goes down? In many cases, no.

6. **Rapport and clear communication are important**. Buying and selling can be stressful. Choosing an agent with whom you communicate clearly and easily will help simplify the process. Be sure he or she understands your needs and expectations and that you understand the process and the agent's expectations of you.

In short, specialized knowledge + quality tools + clear communication = agent who can deliver the results you want in the luxury home arena.

© Laurie Moore-Moore, Institute for Luxury Home Marketing, Dallas (TX), 2002

Broker/Owner or Manager's Checklist

Developing a Luxury Home Marketing Effort For Your Company or Office

STEP 1: Analyze the opportunity

TASK: Gather the statistics for your market place

✓ Identify the top 10 % of properties by price
✓ Determine the total number of listings and closed transactions in the top 10 %
✓ Break the top 10 % of closed transactions into logical price ranges
✓ Calculate the list-to-sale-price ratio for each price range
✓ Calculate the conversion rate
✓ Gather days-on-market for solds in each price range
✓ Determine the number of buyers (closed transactions) by price range
✓ Plot the locations of listings and sales in the top 10 %
✓ Factor in the new home market
    Locate new home developments and plot locations
    Identify prices
    Identify listing opportunities
    Create a builder contact list

TASK: Also answer these questions

✓ What is your market share in the top 10 %?

✓ Does your market share differ by price range within the top 10 %?

✓ Where are your agents listing and selling upper-tier homes?

> Plot sales geographically. Which of your agents are working in the upper tier now? Where do you not have geographic coverage?

✓ What percentage of the upper-tier market do new homes represent?

✓ Is there enough activity (and potential income) to justify an upper-tier program for your firm?

✓ Are there other benefits associated with pursuing the upper tier?

✓ Can you profile the upper-tier buyers/sellers in your market?

> Occupation? Primary or secondary residence? Other key demographics?

✓ What databases are available to you locally?

STEP 2: Evaluate the competition

TASK: Answer these questions

1. What other firms are active in the upper-priced segment?

2. What is the market share of each of the upper tier players? Are some firms stronger in some price ranges? Stronger in resale or new product?

3. How would you define the positioning or image of each of these firms?

4. What are the strengths and weaknesses of each competitor?

5. What vulnerabilities do you see?

6. Is anyone in your market affiliated with national programs such as Sotheby or Christie's Great Estates?

7. Is there a national luxury home program you can affiliate with? Most of the national franchises offer luxury programs and there are several for non-franchised firms including relationships with Sotheby and Christie's Great Estates.

8. Is it possible to acquire an existing upper-tier firm (to buy market share and position) and would it make sense?

STEP 3: Review your company resources

TASK: Analyze your firm

1. What is your image in the market?

2. Do YOU have the time to develop a specific plan to capture the upper-tier market? If not, to whom will you delegate this?

3. What can you budget for this effort?
   What returns do you expect in first 12 months?

4. Can your existing agents handle the transition to the upper tier?
   Which ones?

5. Can you recruit luxury home agents from competition?
   Which agents might you target?

6. Will you depend on agents or add staff to direct and implement?

7. Do you need a luxury home marketing director? Can an existing staff person add this to his/her responsibilities? If so, what will this person's role be? Write a job description.

STEP 4: Develop your luxury home program basics

If your company is part of a national organization, you may be able to adopt and/or adapt the national luxury program to meet your needs. If not, here's a short list of a dozen mind joggers identifying some of the issues you'll need to consider as you develop a program. You'll think of other things, but this will get you started.

1. Know how your luxury home marketing program differs from your competition's and be able to articulate it clearly. Build on this **positioning statement**.

2. **Name** your program.

3. Establish the **minimum price** that qualifies a property for your program. In a large market this may vary by area.

4. Decide what **marketing materials** you need and have them designed and prepared.

5. Define your **commission policies.**

6. Decide **what marketing the company will provide**. How will you charge agents for this marketing? Will the consumer be asked to pay for specialized marketing?

7. Research **additional marketing opportunities** agents may utilize at their expense.

8. Determine what **other policies** are necessary.

9. Decide **who in the firm will coordinate the program**.

10. Build excitement within the firm. Get your agents and managers to buy in to the program.

11. Create a **marketing plan for the program**.

12. Create a **PR plan** and announce the program to the public with press releases. If you have a luxury listing, promote it as the first home eligible for this special program. Choose the home carefully.

STEP 5: Define your objectives and determine how you will evaluate progress

TASK: Answer these questions

✓ What are your goals for the first six months? For the first year? For the first two years?

✓ Projected and actual...

Number of listings you expect?

Number of closings?

Dollar sales volume?

Number of agents participating?

Number of new agents recruited?

Gross commission income earned?

Company dollar expected?

Impact on company's average price?

Budget to develop and implement program?

Sources of buyers?

Target profile of average luxury buyer?

STEP 6: Write Your Plan

TASK: Pull together the answers to all the preceding questions, make the additional decisions outlined below, and put your plan in writing.

1. How will you differentiate your firm in the luxury market?
2. How will you promote?
3. What can you afford to budget? Is this adequate
4. Company contribution to property marketing costs?
5. Company policies for program? Agent splits?
6. What is the task list for implementing your plan to capture the upper tier market?
7. Who is responsible for each task? What are deadline dates?

Laurie Moore-Moore

The Real Estate Intelligence report recently named Laurie Moore-Moore as one of the ten people having the most influence over the real estate industry in the last 25 years.

As co-founder of REAL Trends, Inc. (the well-known research and communications company): For more than 15 years Laurie Moore-Moore has kept her finger on the pulse of today's changing real estate business and provided insight, research, commentary, and conferences for industry participants.

As a national speaker, researcher, and consultant: Each year, more than 10,000 people flock to her presentations on industry trends, luxury home marketing, customer service and sales & marketing. Laurie has personally trained more than 6,000 sales associates and brokers in the marketing of luxury homes.

Known for her research in the real estate industry, Laurie has worked with the National Association of Realtors in the development of popular industry research reports including *Recruiting and Retaining the Best* and the report *What you Need to Know about Today's Home Buyers and Sellers.*

As President of The Institute for Luxury Home Marketing: This exciting new organization offers training, special professional designations, and marketing tools for agents who specialize in fine home and estate properties.

Laurie is a licensed broker and has sold real estate. She has managed a large real estate office, and managed two divisions of one of the nation's largest brokerage firms. She is executive director of an industry CEO group and serves on the Advisory Board of Directors of a Fortune 1000 company.